SO YOU WANT TO WANT TO WRITE A

Other Avon Books by
Lou Willett Stanek

STORY STARTERS
WRITING YOUR LIFE

SO YOU WANT TO WRITE A *Novel*

LOU WILLETT STANEK, Ph.D.

AVON BOOKS ◆ NEW YORK

SO YOU WANT TO WRITE A NOVEL is an original publication of Avon Books. This work has never before appeared in book form.

AVON BOOKS
A division of
The Hearst Corporation
1350 Avenue of the Americas
New York, New York 10019

Library of Congress Cataloging in Publication Data:

Stanek, Lou Willett.
    So you want to write a novel / Lou Willett Stanek.
        p.   cm.
    1. Fiction—Authorship.   I. Title
PN3355.S74   1994   94-14334
803.3—dc20   CIP

First Avon Books Trade Printing: December 1994

AVON TRADEMARK REG. U.S. PAT. OFF. AND IN OTHER COUNTRIES, MARCA REGISTRADA, HECHO EN U.S.A.

Printed in the U.S.A.

OPM 10 9 8 7 6

For my students
with special gratitude to:

Alice Alexious, John Aberth, Jeremy Berman, Colleen Booth, Wayne Brooks, Jim Buss, Gillian Coulter, Ann Marie Cunningham, Lani Dahm, Heather Darling, Anne Dowling, Pat Edwards, Julie Evans, Rona Figueroa, Eric Fisher, Jessy Fuller, Bob Gunn, Terre Hamlisch, Marc Handelman, Marilyn Horowitz, Michelle Louzon, Fran Miksits, Gabe Naimaister, Jim O'Connor, John Oldick, Tony Ortega, Brian Scheuer, Chip Seale, Steven Siegel, Maria Smith, Virginia Swartz, Steve Wittkoff

Contents

Introduction

Of course you want to write a novel. *Stories only happen to people who can tell them.* Hold that thought. Use it as your mantra. Stick with me. You can write your story.

But you have a job, a business, kids, and/or commitments? Most novelists do. I know a Wall Streeter who claims to have written his novel on the subway. A mother in Baltimore wrote hers in the front seat of her Toyota while her kids took ballet lessons, played baseball, became good Scouts. All the members in my writer's workshop—a lawyer, an actress, an accountant, an iron worker, a bartender, a classicist, a mother of four, a secretary, a psychologist, a librarian, a grip, a salesman—have novels in progress. Think of it this way: *if you write one page a day, in a year you will have a novel.* We'll work on a schedule later.

If you're serious about writing a novel, or any type of fiction, you should zip out to buy a notebook before you read any further. A writer never leaves home without one. Ideas pop up at the weirdest times and places but often don't last any longer than soap bubbles. Emily Dickinson composed exquisite poetry on brown paper bags and the backs of receipts, but she created a dreadful mess for the executors of her estate.

The first time I offered a workshop called "So You Want to Write a Novel," a student with eyes the size of shooter marbles looked at me suspiciously and said, "I think you've been reading my mind." The others nodded in agreement. If I've been reading yours, buy that notebook.

Sooner or later, no matter what trade or profession you're in, the urge strikes to cash in your chips and try a different game. Plumbers want to play the tuba, bond traders want to tap-dance, lawyers want to go to sea, accountants want to be sportscasters, mothers want to run IBM, *and everyone wants to write a novel.* This book is an oxymoron, a practical fantasy. It comes with a brown paper wrapper, to protect your anonymity or your other job while you find out if it's possible and if you have the right stuff.

Taxi drivers from New York to Tokyo meet intriguing people. Doctors hear bizarre tales. Business people deal with manipulators. Lawyers' cases take over their lives. Women fall in love with their bosses or each other. Families fight, people get divorced, kids get out of hand. We all have regrets. I challenge a writer to find an airplane seatmate who doesn't have a story he thinks deserves to be told. Most of us want to write a novel to show our sense of the injustice, absurdity, or beauty in the human condition. Material for that story constantly swirls around you.

Nora Ephron's mother, the writer Phoebe Ephron, always told her: no matter what happens, it's copy. Legend has it that on her deathbed she told her daughter to take notes. Nora learned well. When Carl Bernstein had an affair while she was pregnant with their second child, she called gossip columnist Liz Smith and then wrote *Heartburn.*

Phoebe Ephron was right. The first step for a novice is to begin to *think, see, hear, read like a writer.* If your life has begun to seem as dull as a day-old doughnut, here's a way to add a spark. Writers are too busy sleuthing for material to be bored. They notice tics, ties, the shapes of noses, when the copy machine moans, the refrigerator groans. The practice has its dangers. Searching for words to describe how a kiss feels while it's happening can be distracting. Your boss might resent your taking notes while he is in a rage.

People say the funniest things at the sock counter at Saks, do the weirdest things in elevators, airplanes, grocery lines, staff meetings. Make a note. Don't be amazed if the man who sat next to you on the bus this morning—the lardy one in the slick suit that looked as if it had been skinned off a fish— works his way into your story wearing that ghastly suit.

Begetting a character to make you proud is serious business. Find one you can live with for a long time. She'll join you in the shower, read your mail. *Writing a novel is like method acting: when you've found your protagonist, you never come out of character.*

Occupying someone else's skin costs less than plastic surgery and does give you a lift. You read the news from her perspective. She judges the salsa, the Woody Allen movie. She has an opinion about your ex, your mother, the phone call from your boss. Here's another chance to put some zing into your life. It's an exhilarating and spooky experience. You become the person you are creating. Flaubert hadn't had a sex change when he said, "I am Emma Bovary."

What do you need to know about this character? EVERY-THING—his soft spots, mean streak, mood swings, politics, tastes. Would he wear the damnedest gold watch you've ever seen or a Timex? Subscribe to *The Economist, The Nation, GQ,* or *Vanity Fair?* Clip shaving-cream coupons or fly first class even if he had to pay the difference himself? Would she wear perfume to bed alone, burp the baby wearing her good black suit, do whatever dastardly thing it takes to close the deal? How can you find out? By doing the series of exercises in this book, making up your own, living in her skin, digging into your own experience—with caution.

Fact might sometimes be stranger than fiction, and your life might be jazzier than Queen Elizabeth's daughters-in-law's or Milken's at the predators' ball, but even the most beguiling personal experiences don't always make good plots. If you worked your way from office boy to president by being a nice guy or met the perfect mate twenty years ago on a romantic cruise, it's interesting, but it's not a novel. It lacks conflict. Conflict is the *trouble* a character encounters on his way to a happy ending. If Macbeth had won his crown legitimately, Lady Macbeth wouldn't have been a sleepwalker, and we would never have heard of either of them.

Although cutting your story entirely from the material of your life probably won't work, you will use your experience as well as your imagination . . . unless you write with your mother or your wife as the critic in your ear. Let's say your character has encountered a cynical street kid. Your fingers are poised on the keys, ready to have the mouthy dude say appropriately, "Fuck off, lady." Or your character is in the locker room, about to reveal what a shark he is as he tells a colleague about seducing the client's knowledgeable assistant to get the account. But that voice in your head says, Nice girls don't use language like that. . . . What would Aunt Clara think? . . . Will my wife assume I . . . ?

Blink away Mom, Aunt Clara, your wife. Imagine what *The New York Times Book Review* critic will think if the street kid says, "Please, leave me alone, ma'am," or your locker room shark turns into a goldfish.

After you are in character, you'll put on his shoes and see where he takes you. Unless you're the orderly type that alphabetizes her spice rack, don't waste time on an outline. You probably won't follow it anyway, and writing it can be star-studded procrastination. Use the psychic energy for your story. When you know the last line, you're ready to write. Having a destination gives you direction, even if you don't know all the detours. Write in sequence, or you're sure to get lost. The pull and the suspense of your character's quest will drive the book. When your battery dies, jump starts like the following are available all along the way. Pick the ones most appropriate for your story. Writing is a very individualistic art; use this book however it works best for you.

- ☞ WHAT IF nobody gives a damn?
- ☞ WHAT IF there were a leak?
- ☞ WHAT IF she says, "I quit"?
- ☞ WHAT IF he bought cowboy boots?
- ☞ WHAT IF she feels horny and he says he has to spin the lettuce?
- ☞ WHAT IF he felt like nobody after he lost his corporate identity?
- ☞ WHAT IF someone says, "You probably don't remember me. . ." but oh, boy, does he remember?
- ☞ WHAT IF she called it sexual harassment?
- ☞ WHAT IF she were young enough to be his daughter, he had everything to lose, but he wanted her as nothing ever before?
- ☞ WHAT IF the deal fell through?
- ☞ WHAT IF it rained?

"What if" is a fiction writer's magic, but sometimes a single word like "droopy" can tickle your imagination. "Curmudgeon" is one of my favorite site words; with "cur" and "mud" stuck together that way, weird images take shape. And I like the racket the word makes. It sounds old and grumpy. When you begin to think like a writer, enticing words like "duplicitous," "whimper," "pissant," jump off the page and should land in your notebook.

Some books for writers suggest practice lessons, such as writing about how you felt when you lost your skate key, or why you giggled at the funeral, or what you did when he married your sister. You learn to write by writing, but you finish a novel by writing about how your character felt when he lost his skate key, his friend, or the girl.

I suggest warm-up exercises in which you rehearse challenging writing techniques like tapping memory, where atmosphere is more real than incident and nothing is owed to fact, but you never, ever come out of character.

This book offers practical suggestions for moving a story from your imagination to paper. The urge to move my ideas about writing to the printed page grew out of working with novices who proved my theory: writers learn to write by writing. You'll come to know some of them, their problems and successes. Their stories add credence to the theory. I'm convinced if we wrote as much as we speak, writing would be as easy as talking.

The novice who urged me to write this book said the Stanek method is unique, it works. I can't promise you will find an agent or an editor, but if you stick with me and your schedule, I promise you can write a novel. Although I especially address novelists, most of the topics and techniques—character development, using flashbacks, making smooth transitions—apply to all forms of fiction. For good reasons, the most ubiquitous suggestion for all storytellers is still *show, don't tell.*

Let's begin. *Stories only happen to people who can tell them,* a thought scary enough to drive the worst slacker to a typewriter.

CHAPTER 1

Thinking Like a Writer

All my life I had been training to be a writer, unaware. Probably you have too. Writers script reality, for the characters they make up and for themselves. Sometimes it's hard to tell the difference.

As a child growing up on a remote Illinois farm with one horse and no playmates, I had two personae. By day I was Belle Starr, leader of the Younger Gang, riding Wildfire with two red-handled cap pistols strapped on my hips. But at night in the house, when my father "couldn't think straight" if Belle galloped a broomstick horse, I became Brenda Starr, reporting adventures from around the world. I made up the plots, invented exotic settings I longed to see, created the minor characters, and spoke in the voice of the fearless protagonist. I thought I was just playing. Some days as I dash down Madison Avenue, thumbs hooked in my Levi's belt loops, a notebook in my back pocket, I like to think I still have a Belle Starr stride. I know I have a Brenda Starr eye for a story.

So do you, or you will have when you begin to think like a writer. But beware. Writing is addictive. Humorist Fran Lebowitz says she feels as if she's wasting time when she's doing anything other than writing, and that includes tending the sick and going to funerals.

When you begin to think like a writer, you can't turn it off. You will be looking for the details that make the story real, no matter what the circumstance. In a *New York Times Magazine* article, "The Story of a Street Person, Remembering My

Brother," Elizabeth Swados said when she heard her brother had been killed, she kept wondering what kind of truck would run over him in New York City. A Mack truck? A cement mixer? A pickup truck? A van?

Novelists notice how people wear their heels down, show defiance on a crowded bus, get attention, ask people to lunch. They study faces to determine what makes them beautiful, hard, oblivious. Writers read fiction, not only for the story, but also to discover how far away from the central action the story begins, how the author makes transitions, resolves the conflict. When a novelist (you) has a story, she loses her identity to the protagonist.

The first step in becoming a writer is always having your notebook within reach. I've carried one since I was thirteen. The editor of the Vandalia *Leader* gave me the original when he offered me my first job, to write a column, "Lou's Teen Talk," for my hometown weekly in Illinois. "Don't miss anything," was his advice I pass on to you. I took it seriously. The experiences stored in that first notebook became a teen novel called *Megan's Beat*.

The adult novel in my computer today is called *Clipped Wings*. Midwesterners always seem to be trying to get away. Twain took to the river as a steamboat captain. Hemingway went to war as an ambulance driver. I signed on with an airline as a stewardess. Writing the novel, I've learned no matter if the odyssey carries you over the ocean, down the river, or up into the sky, ultimately home will be where you started, even if it's not where you wanted to be or where you will ever live again.

Be prepared. Thinking like a writer could change the way you see and feel about where you came from or where you live.

Toting an accent thicker than suet pudding, Wayne came to New York to become a writer and to shed a small hometown in North Carolina, where people ate moon pies and their speech was sprinkled with idioms like "go to preaching." After a year, reading his work to a group begging for more down-home flavor about people called Chigger and Mama who put on her weddin' dress before hanging herself in the barn, he went back with a tape recorder, a camera, and his notebook. Returning with twenty pages added to his notebook and an album filled with lovely photos of weathered tobacco barns, privies, "crick" beds, hay bales, a barefoot child in a too-long pink dress, and feeling slightly embarrassed by the pride and affection they revealed, Wayne said, "I guess looking at things like a writer does make a difference, doesn't it? I found some things I had overlooked . . . I'm going back in the fall when the tobacco has turned. . . ."

Even if where you came from hasn't been your ultimate destination, a backward look through the sharply focused eyes of a writer might spotlight more than nostalgia. Remember the cousin who made you feel ugly and think your mother dressed you funny? Or the first sale you made . . . those knotty apples you swiped from the tree in your neighbor's backyard? And that spooky alley where you had your first cigarette . . . wonder if it's still as eerie? How would you describe how scary it looked when you were twelve?

You learn to write by writing. It can't be taught, but with a little luck I can train you to be a spy. Writers are spies. When you begin to think, hear, and see like a writer, you will be one, writing a novel won't be as hard as you assume, and your life will be so much more fun.

I wish everyone who wants to write could see *Miracles,* a movie in which two teenagers walk around their Irish seacoast town imagining drama taking place around them, just as it does around you. The boy sees a stranger eating chips. "The drabness of his life was so complete as to have fascination." Write it down, he says to the girl. At first they don't know how to tell a story. They're only noodling, proud of their facility to manipulate ideas and language. But when they become players in separate rites-of-passage stories, they're already thinking like writers. Nothing is lost. At the end, they walk purposefully through total chaos, as if they've found their way through the world's muddle of passions and sensations. *Stories only happen to people who can tell them.*

Writers who welcome you to their world have an eye for the details that mirror real lives, from the liver spots on an old hand to the plastic shower curtain slimy with mold. When your description of the glistening, slick filling and the sour savor of a lemon meringue pie makes a reader's mouth water, you are a writer.

Finding words to describe how things taste takes hard work. But top this: lecturing on a cruise ship, I asked writing passengers to tell me how caviar tasted. "Salty" was not allowed. Most of them moaned, but a man with a cockeyed grin said it was like being kissed by a mermaid.

In New York, where people don't drive, everyone schleps

property, purchases, pets around in shopping bags. What kind and how they feel about their totes are where the material lies. Novelists, as well as dramatists, use props to reveal character. Remember Captain Queeg's ball bearings? Writers notice people who flaunt Bergdorf Goodman bags but hide the cheap drugstore-chain variety under their coats when they shop at Gucci or lunch at La Cirque. I swear people iron the status bags from Tiffany. Walk the streets like a spy. Don't overlook anything.

When luck is a lady, a warm-up exercise becomes a scene, an incident, a chapter, or produces a symbol, a pet, or a minor character who won't go away. In the workshop, there was a dog named Rebel that became the foil for a gutless protagonist, an old coffee mug with cracks that came to symbolize a disintegrating family line, a flower bed whose changing contents from flowers to rocks reflected the health of a love affair.

You might be able to use the exercise about a message on the answering machine to move your story along or for conveying information to the reader. One of the hidden assets for this invention is how it has helped novelists with exposition and with creating tension. Imagine your character hearing the voice of someone who has died, but her voice remains on the tape, or learning he has "quit her" from a recording, or . . .

And don't forget the fax, another high-tech toy. Imagine the guy who faxes his proposal to the woman of his dreams or gives one the size of a DC-10 control panel to his wife as an anniversary present. Then there are the shy characters who find true love through their modems.

Perhaps you are still looking for the protagonist in your story. Exercises will help you to focus on someone who has a tale to tell, a face you like, quirks that intrigue you, idiosyncratic habits that could be a hoot to develop. Even if a dominant character doesn't appear, an exercise starts your fingers working and words flowing. Try these. Keep them in your notebook for future reference.

E X E R C I S E S

∞ WHAT IF your character has a dream? She is dead and is waiting in a long line. When she reaches the front, the admissions angel says, "Do you want to be reborn? You have three minutes to decide." Write her thoughts.

- ∽ WHAT IF, childless, your character and spouse hired a surrogate mother, but she learns that he impregnated the surrogate in the natural way?
- ∽ WHAT IF your character talks to her goldfish?
- ∽ WHAT IF your character appreciated the beeper, but she would've preferred a ring?
- ∽ WHAT IF someone asks your character for the one thing she cannot give?
- ∽ WHAT IF she has to say or hear, "You're fired"?
- ∽ WHAT IF your character feels a frenzied passion for a life he hasn't lived?
- ∽ WHAT IF the dependent child your character raised because he needed love was not such a pleasure when he was still paying the child's bills the day he turned thirty?
- ∽ WHAT IF your character says, "Recapturing one's innocence is impossible"?
- ∽ Your character goes to a Picasso or a Toulouse Lautrec exhibit that affects his dreams. Describe what he sees (blue trees, square women, hefty legs, etc.).
- ∽ Describe a dramatic or bizarre scene where someone makes a marriage proposal. Your character can do it, receive it, remember it, or observe it.
- ∽ In a melancholy moment, your character makes a list of all the people in his life he lets down. (The rest of your novel will slowly reveal why your character can still disappoint them.)
- ∽ Write an incident about an umbrella—one that jabs and stabs, protects, introduces your character to someone, or . . .

Did you learn anything about your character you hadn't realized? Discover one you want to know better? In the first workshop, Virginia discovered humor would define Maggie, her amateur-detective character who sells real estate, when in the dream exercise Maggie peered through the gates of Heaven thinking what a terrific listing it would be.

CHAPTER 2

The Notebook

My friend Judy, who always has her best ideas in the shower, is trying to design a waterproof notebook. Fifteen years ago, a woman with the kind of taste money can buy gave me an elegant red leather one. I haven't used it yet. My words never seem sumptuous enough. It's not a place where you can write, "I'm really pissed off at that sucker."

When I teach a workshop, since a dog-eared mongrel purchased at the grocery store is my only prop, the writers usually acquire one also. I suggest you do too. I never buy a bag or a coat with pockets my notebook won't fit into, or a bedside table that won't accommodate it. The smaller version made to measure for the back pocket of jeans or inside a suit coat works best for men. The spiral allows it to open flat for writing to the edge with ease, but the book's best feature is having five divisions that work like a portable filing cabinet.

A PAGE FOR CHARACTER NAMES

On one cardboard divider, I keep a list of names that might become characters. Try it. Even a name can inspire a story. Updike couldn't seem to stop writing about Rabbit, of all unlikely muses, and look at what Irving did with Garp, a name as poetic as a butcher knife. I was bored stiff after the fourth or fifth time Portnoy masturbated into his sock, but I will never forget his name.

Sally Ride's mother must have had a premonition about where her daughter would travel when she chose to marry a man named Ride.

The not-what-you-expect captures attention. Who can forget Johnny Cash's song "A Boy Named Sue"? I've always had a perverse urge to create a cowboy named Floyd. As we go to press, I'm working on a Southern character whose mother named him Willie Joe, so he chose "William" as his sobriquet.

Even if they haven't read *The Last of the Mohicans,* most people recognize Natty Bumpo, the name Cooper gave his scout in 1826. In the film, Hollywood renamed him Nathaniel Poe, which could help explain why the movie didn't make it through the summer.

When my nephew, Dannon, was a teenager, he told me a tale about his friend the kids called Pealer because he always drove everything fast. He pealed the tires on his trike, his bike, his four-wheeler, and finally, when he was sixteen, his flashy black car with an orange-and-yellow flame shooting down the hood. Under Pealer's name I added "Skeeter," because I liked to say it. For a looooong time a refrain buzzed in my head. "Skeeter and Pealer and me/Skeeter and Pealer and me." Who the devil was "me"? Then one day I heard, "Skeeter and Pealer and me—Bobby Sue." In a flash I knew they were kids who rode the rodeos, and I wrote a story called "Going Down the Road." In Pealer's flashy car pulling a horse trailer, they drove fast down expressways with eight lanes, through cement, high-rise cities. They were singing, "Don't Fence Me In."

Write down the name you would have named yourself. If you have never forgiven your mother for not calling you Courtney, or you see a Zack or a Jonathan when you shave, record it for a character's birth certificate. If you always longed to date just one guy named Chad, or you would've married a woman named Brook, put it in the notebook. Throw in some ghastly names like Herbert too. Not all of your characters will be sympathetic. (Use your head. If Herbert is your cousin's name, family reunions could be tricky after your book is published.) If Percifal connotes class to you, write it down. T. S. Eliot wrote a love song about J. Alfred Prufrock.

When they are good, symbolic names can carry a wallop, but you probably won't win the National Book Award with a prostitute named Angel. Barbara Kingsolver made a lasting impression with the name of a character who never appears in *Pigs in Heaven.* Describing a photo of a mother, she says, "She's already carrying the beginnings of a boy whose name will be Soldier, who will die before he's old enough to fight back." In his book about the FBI, Norman Mailer's calling his agent Harlot might be the best thing about the book. After you name a character Bubbles, there is not much else to do.

E X E R C I S E S

- ○ Think of a name for the person who bullied your character when she was young.
- ○ What name would you give the preacher who bugs your character?
- ○ Your character meets someone whose name is Dallas, Paris, Idaho, Cheyenne, Korea, Dakota, Chelsea, Cambridge, Cherokee and learns why. Write the explanation.
- ○ Your character buys a dog. It is a _____ (breed), which he names _____.
- ○ Your character was once in love with a guy named _____ _____.
- ○ Your character's mother's maiden name was _____ _____.
- ○ In school, they nicknamed your character _____ _____.
- ○ Your character's boss's name is _____, but he calls her _____.
- ○ When she was young, your character played drums with a group called _____.
- ○ Your character once had a car he christened _____ _____.
- ○ Your character chooses _____ as the name for her first child because _____.
- ○ Your character goes out with a woman named _____ _____, who calls her cat Richard Nixon.

No one in the workshop will ever forget Jeremy's Solomon Wise, a character more solemn than wise, or Maria's Blackstone, the corrupt politico who begins his mornings wondering whom he can fuck today.

A PAGE FOR POSSIBLE TITLES

Never underestimate the importance of the title for your story. Titles sell books. I bought Cormac McCarthy's *All the Pretty Horses* before it was reviewed or he won the National Book Award, because this horse lover knew she'd like a writer who would dare to call horses pretty. Titles can have social impact. Look at how Judith Rossner's *Looking for Mr. Goodbar* changed the social habits of many single women, even some who never read the book.

Saint Maybe, the title of Anne Tyler's novel, helps to define the protagonist. The reader must decide if Sue Miller's *The Good Mother* does the same.

Overcoming a killer title can be as hard as writing the book. A critically acclaimed play, *Two Shakespearean Actors* (with a cast of twenty-seven), closed early on Broadway. People on the street said the title sounded like a high school English course. The critics had to do handstands before theatergoers would dash out to see Terrence McNalley's marvelous play *Lips Together, Teeth Apart*. It reminded me of a dentist appointment, and I always wondered if the title of the book *Insomnia, God's Night Course* wasn't designed to cure the malady.

Innumerable writers have borrowed terrific titles from other works of art. The Bible, Shakespeare, and poetry are the sources used most often: *The Sound and the Fury, East of Eden, The Sun Also Rises, For Whom the Bell Tolls, The Grapes of Wrath, Of Mice and Men*. Tom Wolfe's symbolic title *Bonfire of the Vanities* alludes to a story of Girolam Svonarola, a fifteenth-century monk whose crusade against secular temptation won him a huge cult following.

Sense and Sensibility, Great Expectations, Crime and Punishment, Much Ado About Nothing, Jude the Obscure, Tender is the Night, A Farewell to Arms, The Finishing School, A Confederacy of Dunces, Save Me a Waltz, The Wasteland, The Homesick Restaurant, are titles writers wish had been their ideas, but all of the good ones are not used up. Try creating some promising prospects that could be the foundation for a tale. There aren't any rules, even though Hollywood seems to have a list of adjectives and another of nouns they shift around to come up with dull duplications like *Pretty Woman, Pretty Baby, Urban Cowboy, Easy Rider*. If writers followed the formula, we wouldn't have *You Know Me, Al; Even Cowgirls Get the Blues*, or *Death of a Salesman*.

Having always felt as if I were one, I carried the title *Black Sheep* around for three years before finding the story. *Some Things You Never Get Over* has possibilities.

E X E R C I S E S

- ∽ Borrow a word or a phrase from the Bible, or from another piece of literature you love, that could be a possible title.
- ∽ Think of a title using a person's name, like Jane Eyre, David Copperfield, Hedda Gabler, Silas Marner, Rebecca.
- ∽ How might you use a traditional symbol such as the dove of peace in a title?
- ∽ Create a place that could become a title, like Howards End or Wuthering Heights.
- ∽ Imagine a title that will tell what the story is about, like *A Passage to India, Gulliver's Travels*, or *The Return of the Native*.
- ∽ Your character's favorite title of all time is _____ because _____.
- ∽ Think of storylines the following titles imply:

Someone Else's Daughter	*Second Choice*
Better Luck Next Time	*C.J.'s Flunky*
Luck Be a Lady	

Jessy's novel is set in a mental hospital her character calls The Ranch. She draws on irony from several sources for her title, *Home on The Ranch.*

OBSERVATIONS

Writing is a legal way to shoplift. A writer pinches every interesting thing she sees and hears to toss into a treasure chest, her notebook.

Keep your eyes open. Your secretary chews his gum in time with his typing; the cobbler winks at you; the baby winks with both eyes; your date keeps rotating his neck, raising his chin, and he isn't even wearing a tie; lunch looks as if it has been served before; he calls you by her name; her perfume smelled as if it had died. Write it down. You'll probably be able to use it.

What did you notice on your way to work this morning? How people sit on the subway usually conveys their attitude toward their space in the universe. That sullen boy who spread his legs to take up two seats—was he being surly, sexy, or insensitive? Write it down.

In the staff meeting, how did old Charlie let you know, without saying a word, you'd better be on your toes? Figure it out, write it down, and use it for a character as miserable as he. Something good should come out of the hell he has put you through.

Your character is gong to be a redhead, but not the crinkly, carroty kind that comes with freckles on skin so pale the blue veins show. The shade of "an old brick" is as clichéd as "the flame of red hair" in a romance, but you'll recognize the color when you see it. Keep your notebook handy; she might get on the bus or stand next to you in the movie line.

Remember the dress Martha Blake wore to your class reunion? What was it about that dress that made you feel as if you had worn a potato sack? Describe it, put it on your character, and let her knock 'em dead. Writers take their revenge subtly.

⎡E⎤⎡X⎤⎡E⎤⎡R⎤⎡C⎤⎡I⎤⎡S⎤⎡E⎤⎡S⎤

- ↝ Sit in a diner. Notice how three different people place their orders and spend the time until the food arrives. Write it down from the viewpoint of your character.
- ↝ In a meeting, observe how behavior changes when the boss enters.
- ↝ From your character's point of view, describe the tie display in a local department store.
- ↝ Listen to the sounds of the city. Record five, using words that make the sound they describe, like "whine."

∞ Go to a deli. Describe what you see and smell.

∞ Look at the jewelry people wear. Describe the artistic, the fake, the fun, the funky, the junk, the valuable, the heirlooms, and the pieces making a statement—like a gold chain on a hairy chest bared to the belly button, a diamond as big as a cherry chocolate, a gold Rolex big enough to compete with Big Ben. When you're creating your characters, take out pieces for them to wear or flaunt.

∞ At the opera or a concert, record the contortions a performer's body or face goes through to produce the sound.

∞ Sit in a parking lot. Watch the kind of cars people drive. Are their choices predictable? Does "the suit" in a white shirt and rep tie drive a black sedan or a roaring red monster riding as low to the ground as a lizard? Does the glamorous blonde have a convertible she looks good in?

∞ Pull out the family photograph album. How does your dad stand when he has his picture taken? Who doesn't trust the camera? Which cousin always manages to stand in the back row? What do the photos reveal about character?

∞ At a meeting in your company, where do people sit? Does placement denote a hierarchy? Are the rules written or understood? What kind of small talk do the players make before getting down to business? What can cause tension to crackle across the table?

∞ What do the contents of a friend's refrigerator or medicine cabinet reveal that you could use to develop a character in your novel?

∞ You are standing in a grocery-store line. How do the checkers show without saying they are bored with their jobs?

∞ You attend a conference or a training session. One person likes the sound of his own voice so much he can't hush. Record his satisfaction, the leader's frustration, the audience's impatience.

When Jeremy read a disturbing encounter Solomon Wise has in a diner with a troubled Vietnam veteran, the group complimented him on the realism. Jeremy blushed when he admitted the incident had actually happened to him. He shouldn't have. Turning life experiences into art is what writers do.

EAVESDROPPING

When your older sister told you it wasn't polite, she didn't know you were going to be a novelist. Do try to remember those conversations you listened in on when she had such a crush on Joey Smith. You might be able to use them.

You need a cop in your story and you know he doesn't talk like your banker husband? If you live in New York, there is almost always a parade somewhere with a gaggle of cops lining the street talking to one another. Hang around and listen. (Do you like that word—"gaggle"? It's yours. Put it in your notebook. Writers pass it on.) If you live somewhere else, discover where the cops hang out, take a walk, and eavesdrop. It's okay. You're working.

If your lawyer speaks as if his brain has collected a lot of fuzz, the best revenge is to mimic his speech patterns when you're creating a character who has a mind cluttered with nontranslatable, six-syllable words. Put it in your notebook. He can't even bill you.

Be discreet, but when your aunt Clara's conversation could make Miss Malaprop seem like a slacker, write it down. You'll disguise it. She'll never know, and look how Dan Quayle's gaffes turned a faceless senator into the most humorous Vice Presidential character this country has ever known.

Parks, movie queues, coffee counters, buses can be jewel boxes for eavesdroppers, and people say the darnedest things in checkout lines and theater lobbies, but maybe the best pickings can be found at art galleries, especially if the show is controversial.

E X E R C I S E S

- ↝ Collect five snatches of conversation on your way to work. You can fill in the blanks. If you drive, listen to a call-in radio show and use a tape recorder until you can put the items in your notebook.

- ↝ Listen to the messages on your answering machine. Play them again to hear how people talk when they're nervous, disgusted, impatient, angry, whiny, trying to persuade or seduce you. Write them down.

- ☞ Compare the way panhandlers approach people on the street, like the guy who says, "Pardon me, but could you spare a hundred dollars?" and the one who says, "Just enough for some supper. That's all I ask, and the Lord will surely bless you."

- ☞ Truck stops have the best pie, and truckers the best stories. Take your notebook.

- ☞ Go to a bus stop near a high school at 3 P.M. Record the latest slang and fashions before they change again.

- ☞ Don't forget your notebook when you have a dental or doctor's appointment. Write down what the other patients say. Write down the questions the dentist asks when he has the drill in your mouth.

- ☞ When you play tennis, golf, squash, or go to the gym, record what you hear in the locker room.

- ☞ When you visit your perfect friend, the one with the perfect husband, the perfect children, and the perfect house, listen to what she says to make you feel less than perfect.

- ☞ Before you tell your administrative assistant she makes too many personal calls, listen to the language she uses to describe the guy she met at the mall, or how she tells her mother to "get off her back."

Maria's cast of characters spans New York City's political caste system from the borough chiefs to the Mafia. When the voices grow dim, she takes her notebook and walks through the corridors at City Hall.

BORROWED THINGS

Now that you've decided to write a novel, the treasure hunt begins. Store it all in your notebook.

WRITERS READ! They read like writers, and they read everything—fiction, reviews, editorials, columns, travel articles, advertising, business news, the back of the jam jar—and they borrow—political ideas, descriptive details, insights, facts. You need action verbs? Read the sports page. Those guys "slam," "whack," "dunk," "spin." But use your head. They also say things like, "The ball squirted through the legs of Addison."

Rumor has it that advertising lures some of our best writers to Madison Avenue. I had my doubts until I read:

> It was the last summer before income taxes. A young man stood facing the sea, with all the 75-room cottages of Newport behind him. He had nothing to do that day except think about life. A beautiful girl passed him, walked to the end of the dock, stepped aboard a waiting launch and was carried out to sea. Offshore, a brilliant white yacht, measuring 100 feet at the waterline, was waiting. Who knows what actually takes place aboard such boats? The afternoon began with slow thrilling conversation, led to a little lunch of cold lobster and asparagus, and ended with 5 children and 21 grandchildren (every one of them got her eyes, and her money). The girl was 23 that day. It was the first day of her life. Her hair was short and thick and beautiful. She wore an innocent blue "tennis dress" (her sister's) and no makeup. Didn't need any.

The fantasy appeared in a J. Peterman catalog selling a "Newport, 1912 Tennis Dress." Although the clever ad writer eventually revealed his purpose, he set it up as subtly as a novelist, not only establishing the setting in time and place and creating the ambiance of the era, but also sprinkling his story with a touch of suspense until he revealed a happy ending. But pay closest attention to the tone. Even discriminating buying readers will be flattered by his assuming they are as sophisticated and well bred, and have the same sort of refined tastes, as he. Note, also, how the writer bared his aristocratic values as clearly as a flasher in a raincoat. This is not a guy who would enjoy a night on the town at a gin mill with sawdust on the floor and topless dancers on the bar.

As your story unfolds, if it naturally calls for a character with beliefs diametrically opposed to yours, borrow language, opinions, actions from the media, even if you feel they are prejudiced. Bigotry and bias won't be hard to find. But be prepared for your own hang-ups to be exposed. Reading like a writer, you soon realize language and tone will reveal your fictional characters' secrets as well as your own. Discipline and discretion are advised when including hot-button opinions about politics, religion, and social issues while calling it fiction. If the sensation in your stomach feels like a bleeding ulcer when you read First Ladies should know their place, marijuana should be legalized, welfare mothers should work, gays should be sent to Siberia, a soapbox in the park or a letter to the editor would probably be easier and more effective than a novel.

One of the best things about being a writer is how alert you become. Plot possibilities appear in some of the strangest places. Dostoyevsky, always desperate for money, often lifted plots for stories straight out of the daily newspaper. Norma Klein published a novel based on an item she read in an Ann Landers column about a divorced mother who became a lesbian, but my favorite is *The Swap*, the novel she wrote after reading a newspaper account of a young couple who traded their baby for a red Camaro. Barbara Kingsolver, a Southwestern writer, found her idea for *Pigs in Heaven* by watching the controversy over Native American children adopted by outsiders being played out in the media. Faulkner swore *The Sound and the Fury* grew out of an image of a little girl climbing a tree wearing muddy drawers. I recently read a long, touching news article about an innocent teenager, gunned down in the street, who still had a half-eaten Snickers bar in his hand. That sticky candy bar is in my notebook.

A good way for a writer to start her day is to read the newspaper with notebook in hand. As I write this, political columnists in *The New York Times* have overdosed on "sleaze." The sportswriter who calls a boxing event "the match of two bumps on a log" must have had a bad night, but I borrowed "clunked" from a golf story, and "sour, cynical spirit and smirking sadism" from a film review because I'm fond of alliteration, especially with *s*'s. I also recorded a phrase I would never remember—"in vitro fertilization"—because I couldn't stop wondering how a beer-belching stud would feel about having his son conceived in a petri dish. There could be a story there. Then I couldn't stop wondering what "petri" meant, surely not from "petrify." The connotation is grotesque. But the Latin word for rock is *petra* . . . and so it goes when you think like a writer.

What pay dirt did you strike in your paper this morning?

Cookbooks, food and wine columns, travel articles had never been my reading taste until I became a writer. Even though I don't cook much, my characters eat—sometimes in exotic places, and things I've never tasted. Recently, looking for a decadent dessert with a sassy name for a character trying to founder a broken heart, I saw a recipe for Black Pepper and Black Fig Ginger Cake. Having a pepper fetish, I pushed on to find the alliterative Peppered Peaches or Pears in Port. Common sense prevailed before I checked the cupboard for cake tins and peppercorns, but I started thinking about a grandmother character, a sympathetic figure, just a tad eccentric, peculiar enough to put pepper in a cake . . . maybe buy red bikini panties just to see how they felt. She's in my notebook, on the page with a tenacious bulldog called Horatio, who rides in a motorcycle sidecar, I think. I wonder if Granny could drive the motorcycle. . . .

A fiction writer who doesn't read fiction makes as much sense as a Christian Scientist going to medical school. I don't suggest you try to write like James or Joyce or anyone except yourself, but writers do learn from one another. Everyone but Hemingway recognized Sherwood Anderson's and Gertrude Stein's influence on Papa's spare style. Borrowing technique is allowed. If transitions are difficult for you, read how Anne Tyler moves a character from Baltimore to Florida, from high school to thirtysomething, from an interior monologue to conversation with a wacky dog trainer. Write it down.

Richard Linklater's film *Slacker* came from his notebook. For years he had been jotting down curious scenes he'd witnessed and swatches of mad conversations overheard, the sort that all of us try to remember but immediately forget.

John Updike published his notebook. A reviewer said *Odd Jobs* served as a kind of commodious grab bag for the thoughts, observations, and descriptions Updike had never managed to squeeze into a novel. Scraps of experience . . . architecture, women's bodies, the Red Sox, the Fourth of July . . . It was as if he felt a compulsion to document every possible fragment of his life, as though it might evaporate or become meaningless were it not anchored down. Don't let yours vanish. Write them down.

EXERCISES

- ∞ Scan the newspaper for three items that with some inspiration could become a story.

- ∞ Read feature articles, profiles of people who might become part of the composite character you create. Maybe it will be a physical feature of an actor, a character flaw a politician or an athlete shows under pressure, a bigot's remark, an act of courage by a cop or a kid, a criminal's scare tactic, a sleazy lawyer's defense.

- ∞ Make a list of lines of poetry, plays, songs, or speeches your character might allude to when making a point, or you might use to develop her character.

- ∞ Find the names for five chocolate desserts that would make your reader hungry.

- ∞ Look for five off-the-wall words or phrases a columnist uses to describe how a wine tastes. (Prepare yourself for words used in the wackiest ways imaginable. "Smoky bouquet" is only the beginning.) Save the language for someone pretentious, or for a character who is very sophisticated or cosmopolitan, *dahling*.

- ∞ Examine art books. Find a painting your character would buy in reproduction or a poster to hang on his wall.

- ∞ Lift language decorators use to describe rooms, houses, yachts.

- ∞ Scour the travel section for settings.

- ∞ Borrow business talk from the financial pages.

- ∞ Pursue books of photographs. Filch faces and places to put in your notebook.

Steven is a thirtysomething lawyer with no daughters. What does he know about teenage girls' current taste in lingerie? To describe his murder victim's pink teddy, he looked at a picture in *Seventeen* magazine. The women in the workshop said he got it right.

WORDS, WORDS, WORDS

Reserve a lot of space in your notebook to squirrel away words—lists of words—those you don't know, old favorites, workhorses, funny ones, spicy ones, beauties, figures of speech . . . but go easy on the adverbs. "Adroitly" is an impressive word, but if your character has actually said something clever, you won't have to say he said it adroitly. The reader will get it.

When you know your character well, she will begin to own certain words you'll recognize in the theater, in a magazine, overheard on the street corner. Write them down. Scarlett O'Hara laid claim to "sassy," "spunky," "savvy," "scrappy." I don't remember Thurber's using it, but "nerd" belongs to Walter Mitty. Every writer has to feel like a thief when he uses Holden Caulfield's "if you want to know the truth."

In our writers' group, when Virginia's character Maggie has an epiphany, she always says, "Whoa!" One of the other writers read a piece in which he had someone say it, but in chorus, everyone said, "Whoa! That's Maggie's word. You can't have it."

"Dimple" is a word I've been saving. I like the sound and the image too much to give it to a character who doesn't deserve it. "Bingo" and "dumpling" are favorites too, but they're more fun to say than to write.

"Ennui," like "enigma," is a good word but must be used with the utmost discretion. An enigmatic type like Anna Karenina can suffer from ennui, but someone of Madonna's ilk, who wears her underwear and her thoughts on the outside, is better described as being bored as hell.

"Egregious" hits hard if used as sparingly as garlic. Notice how it is necessary to grit your teeth to make the sound. Hoard it for a mega-outrageous situation.

Words know their place. "Splendid" has class. Save it for a glorious occasion. Perky words like "dandy," "ducky," and "dilly" would choke a curmudgeon. "Crabby" and "cantankerous" fit, but not as qualifiers. A "cantankerous curmudgeon" has a ring to it but is as redundant as a "small midget."

I reserve "divine" for something that is, or when I or one of my characters is putting on the dog.

Writers' groups play with words as if they were balls and their team were up at bat. If you want to write a novel, so should you. For example, in a New School workshop, the class had a long debate about what could be the most deadly weapon a murderer could use. They considered an ice pick, a crowbar, a baseball bat, a gun, a butcher knife, but eventually chose a meat cleaver as having a more grisly connotation.

Reserve pages in your notebook for words to describe physical appearance. Translating the image in your mind to a picture the reader sees can be tricky. The color of her eyes and hair is easiest. That's why everyone does it, and you shouldn't unless you can find something more original than cornflowers or sapphires to compare with her blue eyes. Think how lilacs must bore Liz Taylor.

Defects are easier. Bony knees, liver spots, warts, blood blisters, bunions, turkey neck, hammertoe, thick ankles, short waists, a potato nose, are killers. Since literature abounds with bad guys who are missing fingers, it's best to leave yours with a full set. Burly chests and pockmarked faces have also had their day.

The clothes your character wears could be important. Go for a walk with a purpose. Notice what people wear on their feet. I have a closet full of wing tips, cowboy boots, oxfords, biker's boots, saddle shoes, white bucks, thongs, Birkenstocks, clogs, platforms, spikes, slingbacks, bedroom slippers, overshoes, rubbers, Wellingtons. There are sandals, sneakers (not to be confused with tennis shoes), loafers, spectators, and black patent leather pumps for men and women. I add to them constantly and choose carefully when dressing my characters. Remember, Einstein wore bedroom slippers, but Scott Fitzgerald had a proclivity for evening pumps and brown-and-white spectators.

The grandmother who puts pepper in her cake might appear in purple tennis shoes, but the neighbor who wears hose and black oxfords, even in the summer, would never approve. A young Wall Street bond trader would wear sensible heels to the office, but I'd put her in red slingbacks for the weekend.

If you have an executive in your story whom you want to commit political suicide, send him to a board meeting in white sweat socks and penny loafers or put him in short, shiny socks—the kind that shows his hairy leg when he crosses it.

Hats can be props that help to define a character. Remember country singer Minnie Pearl's straw with the price tag hanging down? And look at what Hollywood accomplished by putting a white or a black hat on a cowboy. After World War II, Germany had to design new caps for its police because the old, peaked ones reminded tourists of Rommel's uniform.

Noticing what people wear to cover their heads is just another way to walk through your world thinking like a writer. Make a list for your notebook. Borrow words you need to reveal something about your character's taste, values, status, idiosyncracies.

Mafia boss John Gotti was said to have "whacked" his enemies. In the writers' group, there was a mystery writer, an angelic-looking young woman working on a story about a serial killer of little blond boys, who didn't have any trouble coming up with synonyms. When would the following be more appropriate: "assassinate," "exterminate," "massacre," "kill," "murder," "slaughter," "slay," "cancel," "terminate"? What are your additions?

The word section in my notebook is as cluttered as my closet. I'm recycling many of them into almost every section of this book. Try them on, take what fits or you can use, but my taste might not be suitable for your style. Be on the look-out for bargains of your own. Go ahead, be a conspicuous consumer. Fill your notebook with pages and pages of words. They are still free.

Don't be confused because there is another section called Language. It's not redundant. Words are language, but language is more. It's like comparing a dress with an ensemble. The purpose in this chapter is to raise your word consciousness, to encourage you never to let a good one slip away. Continue to collect them. When you are ready to begin your story, we will spend more time on shades of meaning, value-loaded words, what language is appropriate for what character and what occasion.

When you begin to write your story, you will have to become a ventriloquist.

EXERCISES

- ∞ Read the newspaper. Borrow ten good words you might use later. Pick descriptive ones, powerful ones; those used cleverly, have a pleasant or a weird sound.

- ∞ Make lists of synonyms for the following:

gun	idea	bone
pal	purse	enemy
blush	scream	former spouse
girlfriend	wound	cigarette

- ∞ "Blister" is a hardworking word. Write three different sentences from the viewpoint of your character, using it as a noun, a verb, and an adjective ("blistering").

- ∞ Think of five more hardworking words. "Puddle" and "rotter" are good "ear" words.

- ∞ What sound does a bullfrog make? A tire spinning on ice? A buzz saw? Your telephone at 3 A.M.?

⊛   Sit on a park bench. Watch people's legs. I'm serious. Notice how they walk. Add five more descriptive words to "saunter," "stroll," "shuffle." You will have young and old characters to develop in your story. Watch the baby who still finds taking a step tricky business, the ten-year-old who never seems to touch the ground, lovers who look like centipedes.

⊛   Showing a character's fear creates suspense. Make a list of things that frighten your character. In your story, which would be the most effective: "frightens," "scares," "spooks," "terrifies," "terrorizes," "alarms," "unnerves"?

⊛   Walk around your neighborhood noticing plants, flowers, and trees. Ginkgo—a tree having not only interesting yellow fanshaped leaves, but also a nice sound—is a delicate lady, but the ailanthus is a tough guy who grows on a junky vacant lot, through the cracks in the sidewalk, or in the shade of the projects.

⊛   List colors other than primary ones. I swear, this summer a young man turned up in my workshop whose hair had been colored with mulberry juice. Use adjectives if you need them to get the right shade. Since movie star Jessica Lange is all eyes, you would have to describe them. "Buckeye brown" could work. I have a cousin who has butter-yellow hair.

⊛   Go to a gourmet food shop. Collect food for your character to eat. Make lists of the different cheeses, breads (don't forget the shapes—twists, knots, half a beach ball, etc.), teas, fruits (include the colors), varieties of lettuce (the character who prefers iceberg would never marry the person who has to have arugula).

⊛   Comparisons can be effective if they are used as sparingly as eye shadow. Clichés are poison. Forget "teeth like pearls," "mad as a hornet." "She made him as comfortable as a blistering sunburn"; "her boss was as compassionate as the IRS," might do. See if you can create something interesting with the following:

her voice was like _____   *a friend like* _____
shy as _____   *a mind cluttered as* _____
_____ *like a sunflower*   *the call hurt like* _____
a pink slip _____   *death is* _____
a briefcase _____   *his son reminded him*
                    of _____

∽ Edit the following:

"I hate you," she said angrily.
"I love you," he said with feeling.
"Buckle your seat belt," he said protectively.
The boom box blared loudly.
"You've got a cute little butt," he smiled.
Her eyes dazzling and shiny as Tiffany diamonds reminded him of a sparkly day in summer, like the ones he had known as a child, when the world was as bright and brilliant as a new dollar or new-mown hay.

The right word for the right image creates a picture as lasting as a photograph. In the workshop, Alice's sophist from antiquity drinks his wine from a krater, but in North Carolina, Wayne's characters drink their Cokes out of the bottle, and they drop in salted peanuts.

CHAPTER 3

The Schedule

Plan your writing schedule in nonerasable ink. If you really want to write a novel, honor your schedule the way you do an obligation to arrive at work on time or keep a dental appointment. If you don't write regularly, it's like not keeping in contact with a friend. You forget things, lose interest, and it takes too much time to get back to where you were. Writing every day can be a healthy and productive habit, because you do learn to write by writing. Trust me.

Making time to write regularly, even if it means giving up something like jogging, an extra hour of sleep, lunch, watching TV, or talking on the phone, is essential. The most drastic case I know is the writer who removed her kitchen appliances and turned the room into an office. I'm not suggesting you go to such extremes, but thinking about writing, maybe, when you can find the time or feel inspired, will not produce a novel. Count on it.

Whatever works is the right schedule. Choosing the time when you are at your best—early morning, after midnight—is crucial. Let your body rhythms dictate your schedule. There is no absolute, magic hour, only yours. My writing schedule starts at 5:30 A.M. I plant blue morning glories outside my study window. By early afternoon the flowers and I fold up. Writers' work agendas vary as much as their material.

Hemingway wrote (standing up) every day from early in the morning until his first drink. When Barbara Wersba begins a story, she never gets out of her pajamas. Rumor has it that when Erica Jong ends a romance, she begins a novel. Richard Marek, a busy publishing executive, got up earlier, wrote one page every day. In a year he had finished his novel. Five days a week, for over twenty years, Norma Klein wrote ten pages every morning and then went out to lunch or the movies. She published thirty-nine books.

In *Becoming a Writer*, Dorothea Brande recommends writing from the moment you open your eyes, as a way of capturing the subconscious. She must have met a lot of writers like me, who couldn't write their names without a cup of coffee. Put it in a thermos the night before, she advises.

After you have a character who has a story to tell, you will feel cheated or frustrated when your schedule is interrupted, but I hope not to the extent of Kafka, who wrote to Max Brod:

> Writing sustains me, but is it not more accurate to say that it sustains this kind of life? By this I don't mean, of course, that my life is better when I don't write. Rather it is much worse then and wholly unbearable and has to end in madness. But that, granted, only follows from the postulate that I am a writer, which is actually true even when I'm not writing, and a nonwriting writer is a monster inviting madness.

Even with other obligations, there are ways around being a nonwriting writer. If you have a full-time job or career working in an office, teaching, practicing law, selling from your car, writing where you are already used to producing might work. Pack a sandwich, close your door, and have a writing lunch. Wallace Stevens stayed late in his insurance office to create his poems. Coming in an hour earlier when you have solitude, silent phones, access to a computer or a typewriter, could be a good idea.

After a busy or a lousy day, instead of watching predictable sit-coms or playing a vicarious game of football from the couch, writing for a couple of hours could work like the sherbet the French use to clear their palates between courses in a meal.

Writing has been known to be good therapy. Look at the Fitzgeralds. Zelda wrote *Save Me a Waltz* in a mental hospital. After a very long drunk, F. Scott was reported to have said he wrote *The Crack-up* to keep it from happening to him.

If your work requires travel, airplanes—where you can't be

interrupted by the phone or your kids, spouse, friends, boss, or colleagues—can be the perfect place to write. Talking your ideas for revealing character or developing a scene into a tape recorder as you drive along your territory or wait to see a client keeps the story alive until you can sit down at the typewriter again.

Meg Wolitzer is not the only college student who has developed work begun in a creative writing class into a published novel.

Several mothers in my workshops have taken their children's nap time for their writing period, and I notice many parents at the playground, notebook in hand.

To see if you have the right stuff to be a writer, analyze how you spend your time, how you might be more efficient, when you are most energetic. Set a reasonable schedule. Keep it. Try to build in time to read your work with other writers.

When you have trouble starting, do the warm-up exercises found at the end of every chapter. I've yet to work with a writer who hasn't used material from warm-ups in his novel, but don't worry about a rash of duplicate stories. I was amazed at the diversity of responses to "Your character is pulled over for speeding." A CEO was driving her own limo; as the handsome cop approached her car, a young woman— who wasn't carrying her driver's license—checked the mirror to see how she looked; a guy dropped the fifty he was trying to fold behind the license . . .

E X E R C I S E S

- ∞ I will write approximately _____ hours from _____ to _____.
- ∞ I will write (days)_____.
- ∞ To meet this schedule, I will have to (eliminate, rearrange)_____.

If you continue to find excuses not to work, your resistance must be stronger than the urge to write. Perhaps you should try something else, like tap dancing or fly-fishing. Daydreaming is only part of the creative process.

CHAPTER 4

Where to Work, What to Wear, and Other Tips for Keeping the Momentum

The independence is what most novelists like best about their lives and their work. No one tells you when, where, what, or how. You make the rules. Indulge your quirks. If your words will flow only through #2 yellow pencils, sharpen a lot of them. If papaya juice arouses your creativity, stock up. Fiction writers have found worse stimulants. The following suggestions have worked for some writers. Feel free to filch what works for you.

WHERE TO WORK

Set up shop someplace that doesn't require a construction crew each morning—your desk, the dining room table (if you usually eat in the kitchen), a card table in your bedroom, basement, barn, attic, woodshed. Finding a place where you won't have to tidy up for company will save much time.

If you live in an infamous New York closet apartment, a lap desk that will fit under the bed, next to the stepladder, beach chair, and box of out-of-season clothes, can work. In Lake Forest or Shaker Heights, a bed might simply be a piece of

furniture, but in Manhattan, a futon has been known to function for five rooms and a hall closet. I know people who eat,
read, write, mend, watch TV, pay their bills, drink wine, do
their taxes, make love, talk on the phone, give themselves
pedicures, and entertain friends on their beds.

In the movies and in photo essays in magazines like *Vanity
Fair,* high-roller writers like Barbara Cartland and Judith Krantz
usually seem to write propped up in a bed fitted with pink silk
sheets, on one of those fancy wicker breakfast trays. Maybe I'm a
cynic, but I always think the props department brought the frilly
bed jacket and the tray for the shoot, and when the camera is off,
those women write with a yellow pad on their knees, or get up and
turn on their computers like the rest of us.

Natalie Goldberg, author of two excellent books on writing
(*Writing Down the Bones* and *Wild Mind*), doesn't walk you
through the steps for completing a novel, but she makes "living
the writer's life" as appealing as her writer's voice. She and her
friends meet to write in cafes. I can't imagine writing a novel with
a companion drinking caffe latte across the table, but it can be a
terrific place to fill up your notebook or do warm-up exercises. In
my workshops, the way the writers work is as diverse as they are.
After writing around and around her idea, Gillian finally found
her story and told the group she couldn't even stand having the
cat in the room while she worked, but Jim and Jessy write together once a week. Working my way through a master's degree
flying for United Airlines, I wrote tomes on Spenser's *Faerie
Queen* and Henry James's *The Golden Bowl* at coffee counters
around the world, but when I'm working on a novel, my character
and I stay home.

WHAT TO WEAR

Many writers can't write a word until they look like a professional down to the tie, earrings, and perfume, while some of
us became writers so we would never have to wear panty hose
in July and August again. My muse resides in the pocket of
a dilapidated blue terry-cloth robe my cleaning lady once
tried to cut up for dust rags. I have never written a printable
word wearing shoes.

Clothes as white as a blank page were trademarks for Mark
Twain, William Faulkner, and Emily Dickinson. You can tell from
his language Henry James wore a stiff collar. Children's book

writer Norma Fox Mazer still wouldn't own anything but jeans, if her daughter hadn't demanded Mom wear a dress to her wedding.

Make yourself comfortable and write.

A POTPOURRI OF PREREQUISITES

- ↝ Keep your supplies collected—coffee mug, dictionary, paper, eraser, ribbons, cartridges, wits, worry beads, etc. Reluctant writers can fritter away most of their schedule searching for a pencil sharpener or an extension cord. If you write on the subway, try to find a seat and carry a yellow pad.

- ↝ In my opinion, after spellcheck software, laptop computers are the most fabulous inventions since the lead pencil and the yellow pad. Many of us have one longer arm from lugging the first heavy portables around the world. Now I write on airplanes, subways, my terrace, at the beach, in people's guest rooms, coffee shops, the park, without having to follow up with a massage. I haven't thrown away my notebook, but when they invent a laptop to fit in my back pocket, I might.

- ↝ Working on a computer, typewriter, or yellow pad is your call. You make the rules. Many writers start on the yellow pad, scratch out, mark through, scribble in the margins until they have something respectable to put in the computer. Terre says seeing the squibbles and the corrections makes her feel as if she is a hardworking writer. My corrections have all been eaten by the computer. It has been so long since I've handwritten anything, I can't even scrawl a quick note to my sister. "Writers have to suffer" is an old wives' tale. Make it as easy for yourself as possible.

- ↝ No matter how you write, MAKE COPIES. While switching systems, my new machine devoured the first fifty pages of a novel I'm convinced was the best thing I've ever written. Tony left his briefcase on the subway. He lost his novel, his notes, and for a long time his incentive. The gossips have said Hemingway had his first affair after Hadley left a suitcase full of his short stories on a train.

∽   Remove distractions from your workplace—your lover's or your child's photo, your mother's unanswered letters, bills, your briefcase from the office, the cruise brochure. If you face a bulletin board, tack up a magazine photo of someone who resembles your character, a shot of the setting you're trying to create, a person going through a motion you want to describe, like a runner, or a skipper hoisting a sail. If you work like Charles Dickens, you'll want a mirror. According to his daughter who secretly watched him work, he would run to the mirror, grimace, smile, look surprised or shocked, then dash back to record what he had seen. Jim has been known to ask Jessy to strike a pose while he records how she looks.

∽   Science has proved there is no connection between creativity and food, nicotine, or caffeine. Exceptions exist for most laws.

∽   Tell your friends and family your writing schedule. Explain it's nothing personal, but you won't be available for chats or phone calls between, say, 8 to 10 P.M. All of them won't pay attention. Buy an answering machine. Turn it and your typewriter on simultaneously. You will know you are a writer when HE calls or SHE calls and you keep typing.

∽   Think about your story, even in your dreams. WRITE REGULARLY. A lapse means loss of momentum, memory, and motivation.

∽   Quit for the day when you still have something to say, knowing where you are going to begin next time. Playing it out in your mind for a day is apt to enrich the scene. Keep the notebook handy for a brilliant idea, a cogent bit of dialogue, the perfect detail.

∽   Begin each day rereading a portion of the story. What you wrote the previous day is probably enough. It's a chance to do some proofing while jogging your memory. A perverse imp will tempt you to reread the entire manuscript every day. He will also suggest you are hungry, would like a beer, have to pee, should call your broker, return Harry's lawn mower, clean the venetian blinds. His name is Procrastination.

CHAPTER 5

Finding a Soul Mate

(If you are a born loner, writing this novel is your secret, and you plan to keep it confidential, skip to the next chapter.)

Writers and long-distance runners have much in common—discipline, competition, a long haul, delayed gratification, and loneliness.

Finding a person with a generous nature is the answer, whether it be an instructor or another writer. No Svengali need apply. A giver who sincerely wants you to succeed will not view your success as taking anything away from him. It's pretty silly for a teacher to be intimidated by a student who writes like an angel. His being overly critical, callous, cynical, or inattentive, or setting absurdly high standards, will neither diminish the student's talent nor increase his own. Most of us who teach soon realize we will often face our betters, armed only with experience. The secure ones find reflected glory gives off light.

The instructor sets the tone for the students' responses. A writing class should also hone your critical-thinking skills. You'll know you're in a good class when the reader moves into the author's chair, and the teacher says the reader is not on trial, but the critics must prove they can be as objective as a jury by noticing what is well done, as well as what needs work. Most would-be writers will come with a critical ear, but a leader can offer suggestions about what to listen for, like descriptive details that reveal rather than judge, exposition that doesn't go on too long, actions and dialogue that show, not tell, motivation. She can also suggest writers begin with what they liked. The group won't stay together long if she doesn't.

If you are taking a class, a good way to begin is sharing gems from your notebook. The prospect of having to read to your colleagues makes you as alert as a palace guard wherever you are, and the class peppier. When you have a character and a story in progress, members will bring things you can use—"I saw this man at the ballpark who reminded me of the way you described your character, Sam, in the scene you read last week. Instead of watching the game, the man read a science fiction novel and twisted his hair. Use it, if it works."

If you are working on your own, try to find or form a writers' group or at least search for one fellow traveler—someone at work, a friend, a member of your family, who would be willing to meet with you. Even George Eliot said, when she was writing, she needed someone to tell her she wasn't a noodle.

Before you read the work you've done on your novel, do some of the warm-up exercises together, as you do at the gym. Write for ten minutes (always from the viewpoint of your character, of course) about a sourpuss, a regret, a memory, a member of your character's family. Tackling the same task, but approaching it from a completely different perspective, increases your sensitivity to voice, point of view, tone, character. If your protagonist is a grumpy grandfather in a retirement community and your soul mate is writing from the viewpoint of a forty-year-old woman running for mayor of Topeka, their reactions to a sourpuss should be a tad dissimilar.

Reading your work aloud helps you become a finer self-editor. Other people's reactions give you an idea about pacing, the emotional impact of your tale, the appeal of your character. No matter how supportive or polite the group, when you've gone on too long with dialogue in a scene, told them more than they ever wanted to know about a setting, given information they've heard before, started too far away from the action, written around and around the issue, they'll squirm, doodle, go blank-faced. If you've built a noncompetitive atmosphere, they will offer opinions, and give suggestions, but do it kindly.

ETHICS

Let's talk about ethics for writers' groups. Writing is not like a tennis match or a Monopoly game. The goal is not to beat the other guy. The main purpose is support! People pay more attention when you offer criticism in a suggestive spirit. Tearing down others' confidence doesn't give you a dab of your own. The prime principle in a writers' group is to point out what works as well as what doesn't.

You come hoping the others will think your work is wonderful. They come for the same reason. Everyone is entitled to his opinion, but that's all it is, an opinion. Twenty-eight editors were of the opinion William Kennedy's work wasn't worth publishing, until Viking published *Ironweed* and it won the Pulitzer Prize. William Golding's *Lord of the Flies* was rejected twenty-one times.

A bright, involved, energetic member's strength can be his weakness if he is perceived as too competitive, if he wants to carry the critic's ball every time, if he offers an opinion as though it were an umpire's ruling.

His counterpart is the one who idles in neutral until it's her turn to read. To take, you have to give. It's only fair.

A time-hog can destroy a group. Setting a limit in the beginning as to how many pages, how much time each writer has for his work, will take care of everyone except the "I am the center of the universe" type who never looks at his watch or the others' faces.

Most writers who join groups are not only serious about their work, but usually have other commitments, responsibilities, and jobs. Kibitzing long after the others are ready to go to work will be received with the same warm reception as gossiping during an ardent bridge game. People who come to talk about their kids, their spouses, their wardrobes, their bosses, should be encouraged to join the PTA, see a marriage counselor, hire a personal shopper, or visit a head hunter.

Writers are fragile, can be easily hurt, especially regarding their work. Some have been destroyed. There's an ironic moral in John Kennedy Toole's story. His *Confederacy of Dunces* sold to a respectable house, but things went wrong and it was not published. After seven or eight years of agony, he committed suicide. His mother, a very determined lady, devoted the rest of her life to seeing that book in print. Persistently she tried the usual channels, to no avail. Finally she took the manuscript to novelist Walker Percy, a kind man who could not resist her tenacity. He agreed to read the manuscript, later admitting he had planned to read the first chapter and write her a nice, consoling letter. But, captivated by the biting satire and the humor, he read the story in one sitting. With Percy's recommendation, the book not only was published, but is still in print.

CAMARADERIE AND OTHER STICKY WICKETS

When a group clicks, however, the writers' affection for one another can hinder development. Separating a person from his work is as hard as skinning a squirrel.

For a bunch of Yankees, hearing anything beyond the melody of a sweet Southern accent is almost impossible. When I realized Wayne could read IRS instructions and we would find them enthralling, I asked him to leave a copy of his work for me to read sans his Carolina inflection. Many of the others in Wayne's group had impressive résumés, like Alice's Ph.D., Eric's and Steven's law degrees. Ann Marie had written a best-selling biography. Lani was an accomplished actress, Bob a psychologist. Later there was Rona, who played the lead in a Broadway musical, and Terre, a TV personality who was married to a famous musician. Yet the credentials, accomplishments, and connections were not as intimidating to their fellow critics as the group's camaraderie.

Stories abound about friendships and rivalries writers have formed at The Iowa Workshop, Yadoo, in local writers' groups, writing classes. One of the best is Cynthia Ozick's 3/30/92 *New Yorker* article, "Reflections (Alfred Chester's Wig)," in which she considers the effect on her life and work of having known Chester, a hairless writer who died relatively young and tragically before he achieved his literary growth. It's also about Mr. Emerson, their teacher at NYU, who, Ozick remembers, specialized in "sarcasm, parody and a kind of thrilling sardonic spite." Mr. Emerson—so the story goes—stepped into a wood and shot himself the summer following his having set off the sparring between Chester and Ozick she describes this way:

Chester and I were roped-off roosters, or a pair of dogs set against each other—pit bulls—or gladiators, obliged to fight to the death. All this was Mr. Emerson's scheme—or call it his vise or toy—arbitrarily settled on after the first assignment . . .

Although Mr. Emerson encouraged envy, Ozick thinks the teacher suffered from his own envy. "It is not unheard-of for older would-be writers to be enraged by younger would-be writers," she says. In spite of Mr. Emerson's encouraging the savagery of competitiveness between them, what came out of it besides jealousy was fraternity, according to Ozick. She loved Chester, the first real writer she had ever known.

Ozick's love for Chester was platonic, but the chances of a romance flourishing in a writers' group are much higher than of being hijacked on a jet. The first hint is when two members of a group name minor characters after each other and become flustered when the others notice. If what you really like to do is write or talk about writing, the odds are against meeting your heart's desire in a cooking class or at a Mets game.

Groups give you pleasure. They also give you material. TV actor and writer Jerry Seinfeld says he gets his dialogue and situations from "hanging out with my friends." The Brontë children might have lived isolated lives, but they had one another. Emily is assumed to have modeled Heathcliff on the dark side of her brother, Patrick Branwell. Writing a novel personifies delayed gratification. Writers without a group can feel like Vladimir or Estragon waiting for Godot to validate their existence.

But beware. If James Joyce had read the manuscript for *Finnegans Wake* in our group, I'm afraid I would've suggested he see a shrink.

E X E R C I S E S

- ∽ To find other writers to meet with, I will _____ _____.

- ∽ What I want from a group is _____.

- ∽ I will set aside time to read my work and hear others (once a week, twice a month, every summer in a workshop) _____.

∞ We will meet at my house, in a coffee house, or
   _____.

∞ Ground rules I hope to set are _____.

Heather and Tony have gone back to finish their degrees. They said gaining confidence from the writers' group gave them courage. Jessy decided if she could create a character on the page, she could do it on the stage. She took acting lessons. We all went to see her first play. She was a star.

When Wayne's cat died, he got to read first. When Alice's mother-in-law came from Greece to spend two weeks, Alice went first. Steve is a criminal lawyer. The week his client hanged himself on the witness stand, the group took care to avoid being judge and jury in the workshop.

CHAPTER 6

Getting Over the Hurdles

Finding a character you understand, whose story you want to tell, presents the greatest trial for a beginning writer. If you have stuck with the task to this point, surmounting other hurdles should be as easy as not stepping on a crack in the sidewalk.

I list obstacles that have bothered other writers, not to plant negative ideas in your head, but to talk you out of them if they have crept into your thoughts. If you are on a roll, skip to the next section.

- ☞ failing to keep your schedule
- ☞ thinking there are rules everyone knows but you
- ☞ failing to take charge
- ☞ fearing exposure
- ☞ replacing doubt with confidence
- ☞ writing for the wrong reasons
- ☞ trying to write like someone else
- ☞ giving up hope too soon
- ☞ failing to understand your character's motivation

FAILING TO KEEP YOUR SCHEDULE

Miracles have happened, but never in the history of civilization has a story been written by divine intervention. If you want to write a novel, you make it a priority and arrange your life and your time to accommodate your writing schedule. When a wannabe writer finds himself watching TV, sleeping, calling up a friend, doing chores that could wait, during the time he has set aside to write, chances are he hasn't found a character who interests him very much. Compelling characters drive you nuts, won't let you rest until you tell their tale.

Inspired by a series of drawings depicting Lord Nelson's illustrious naval career, Susan Sontag switched from essays to a novel set in the eighteenth century, wrote twelve hours every day, and felt bereft when the story was finished. M. E. Kerr says when she was a child her mother was the biggest gossip in town. After she made her daily rounds collecting the news at the beauty shop, the diner, etc., Kerr's mother called her friends, always starting with, "Wait till you hear this. . . ." Kerr says she knows she has a story when she sits down at the typewriter thinking, Wait till you hear this.

If you don't think the world is eager to hear your story, don't give up. Find one that will set your readers on their ears. Put your character in a different career path. The great novel revealing the quirks and conflicts of the corporate world hasn't been written. Digging into what drives or defeats an athlete could be an interesting story. Friendship is a bottomless theme . . . movie directors have explored camaraderie between women, but you might be the one to write the definitive novel. Your boy-meets-girl could be like no other.

THINKING THERE ARE RULES
EVERYONE KNOWS BUT YOU

Unless you plan to write a pop culture story, like a Western or a romance, which has a formula, the only rules are *credibility* and *clarity*. The rest is appeal. The reader must believe the character could be a real person and the story actually might have happened, or your story must be so appealing the reader is willing to suspend disbelief, as we did when we accepted fairy tales as children or read about aliens from outer space. Although scholars have spent lifetimes trying to untangle *Finnegans Wake,* usually a reader demands clarity—knowing where the scene is taking place, who is talking, why characters are behaving as they are.

No matter what some writing books or some teachers tell you, the only rules are *make it credible, make it clear, make it compelling.* Books and instructors can show you how to punctuate tricky dialogue, give you advice on technical questions—such as how often to identify a speaker when two characters are talking—and suggest smoother transitions, but it's your story. You make your own rules for telling it.

Look at what some well-known novelists have gotten away with. Jane Smiley's *A Thousand Acres* is *King Lear* set on an Iowa farm. Harold Brodkey's characters make love for a hundred-plus pages in *The Runaway Soul.* Martin Amis's *London Fields* is a tale told backward. The central figure starts by dying, ends by being conceived. Alice Munro's short story, "Carried Away," skips back and forth in time from World War I to the fifties—sometimes from paragraph to paragraph without transition other than character names.

FAILING TO TAKE CHARGE

Rebels make the best novelists, the take-charge types who don't like to be told what to do. If you have always worked in a bureaucracy where orders have been passed down a chain of command, it could take some adjustment for you to realize no one will tell you what or how much to write. Most important, there is not a soul to give you a form to follow. A manual of style tells you where to put commas, not how to develop a unique style. You rely on your experience as a reader of good literature and your own instincts as a storyteller. Decisions come after an internal debate: would it be more effective to let it be known immediately your character's father is in prison, or should you build tension by having her be mysterious about her family background until a crucial scene where her secret is exposed? The writers in your group, a spouse, a roommate, or a teacher has the right to an opinion, but you know much more; it's your story, your decision.

FEARING EXPOSURE

Forget about it. Of course readers are going to know how you see the world. So what? Whether you realize it or not, you've been exposing your beliefs, attitudes, values every day of your life, just as your characters do when they speak, make decisions, choose friends and careers. You probably have less to hide than you think. Fitzgerald's fascination with the rich was evident long before he wrote a story. Forster, obviously homosexual, need not have withheld publication of *Maurice* until after his death.

If someone who matters to you could be hurt by your using her actual life experience in your story, who said your book had to be confessional? Transform it, change it, disguise it, or find other material that makes a similar point. If you cheated on your wife and want to show how guilt can eat away your insides until you no longer feel you deserve anything, the power of guilt is your subject. Make your character culpable for some other crime or infraction. It'll probably be a better story. A writer with some distance between himself and his character can see farther and more clearly.

REPLACING DOUBT WITH CONFIDENCE

The majority of people in the universe would like to write a story. Stand tall. You're doing it. If you don't feel you're doing it as well as you would like, remember you learn to write by writing. Trust me. If you want proof, read Faulkner's first novel, *Soldier's Pay,* and compare it with *The Sound and the Fury.*

WRITING FOR THE WRONG REASONS

Eric, the overworked lawyer who gets up early to write two pages to read in the workshop, says he writes for the love of doing it, of finding the words to put on the page. That's the only reason to write.

The people who bought this book thinking writing a novel was a shortcut to fame, money, or getting revenge have probably sold it to a used-book store by now. Writing is hard work. It takes incredible discipline and dedication. Someone who doesn't like to read stories and isn't fascinated by the power and beauty of language, who can't become heady over a well-turned sentence, probably should try wine tasting or rollerblading.

TRYING TO WRITE LIKE SOMEONE ELSE

Wearing men's trousers won't give you Katharine Hepburn's style, any more than following Judith Krantz's formula will land you a seven-figure contract.

When I first started to write, Julian Bach, a very practical man who represented writers like Theodore White and Judith Rossner, was my agent. One day when I was explaining a story I wanted to write, he pitched a Danielle Steel paperback to me. "To support your habit, write something like this that sells," Julian said. "Then you can afford to work on being as literary as Virginia Woolf."

I read the first paragraph, told from the viewpoint of this gorgeous blonde who said her long legs went on forever. "Sorry, Julian, my typewriter won't say that," I replied. But I don't know a writer who on a dark day hasn't tried to parody those incredibly successful escapist writers. It can't be done. I assume Steel sincerely believes in what she is writing. Maybe she is lucky enough actually to think a woman can climb over a few anthills to find waiting on the other side a sensitive, sexy, handsome, wealthy man of her dreams, who adores her. Those of us who think such a situation is as likely as making it to the top of Mount Everest barefoot try to do it tongue in cheek, and our spoofs are as transparent as cellophane. Great writing comes from conviction.

Hammett, Hemingway, Salinger, and, lately, Raymond Carver and Anne Tyler have inspired schools of imitative writers, but the emulators don't make it into *The Oxford Companion to American Literature*. Trust your own voice. Assuming a new one is as unlikely as Sinatra sounding like Pavarotti. I think the telephone has hindered the development of writers' voices. A letter writer develops a style and a voice while doing practical chores like settling an insurance claim or describing the renovated kitchen to his mother in Keokuk.

GIVING UP HOPE TOO SOON

Remember when you started taking piano lessons? Remember the music you were trying to play when you quit? If you had it to do over again, would you give up?

Maybe you have already written the first chapter of your novel, and it went smoothly, but you can't keep up the momentum. Perhaps you summarized your entire story at the start. Beginners sometimes do.

I will be talking more about structure later, but for now, remember a novel has three parts—a beginning, a middle, and an end. The first part is exposition, the introductory material, which creates the tone, gives the setting, introduces the characters, and supplies facts necessary to an understanding of the story. It doesn't give away how the conflict will be settled, how the story will end.

FAILING TO UNDERSTAND YOUR CHARACTER'S MOTIVATION

If you are stuck, it could very well be because you still haven't come to understand the grounds for your character's actions. This especially happens when the character is based too closely on your own personality and experience.

For example, you might have created a protagonist who cannot abide taking orders from anyone—his boss, his wife, the IRS—but you can't face or haven't dug deep enough to discover why he has this temperament. Remember, the base for your character's behavior lies in his moral nature and personality. When you understand his motivation, his actions will be clear and consistent, whether your readers agree or approve or not. He can remain static or he may change, but he shouldn't break off and act in a way that is not in keeping with his disposition.

Don't let hurdles spook you. If you have an intriguing character, the two of you will find a way over or around them.

CHAPTER 7

Your Character

Creating a character won't be difficult. Think of the experience you have had.

When you have a new boss, you meet an eligible someone at a party, a new member joins your club or organization, a new neighbor moves next door, your brother drops in for dinner with a new date, you hire a new employee or baby-sitter, your child introduces you to the person she is going to marry, you change barbers or hairdressers, what do you try to detect immediately? Make a list of the things you want to know about these people.

That list is a start for what you will have to learn about your character. You will certainly want to know if you can trust your boss, how the eligible someone feels about his mother, if the new member of your group is a giver or a taker, if the neighbor is nosy, if your brother's date likes Chinese take-out, if the new employee resents authority, if this person who is going to marry your child has a mean streak, if your barber is a Yankees fan. You have to grasp all those aspects of your character—and more.

What do you need to know about your character? Enough to write her biography. Actors call it the *backstory*. Who and where was the character before the curtain opens? Knowing what has happened to her before your story begins will be the energy propelling your novel.

Even if a match is never struck in your plot, you must understand how your character would behave in a burning theater and why. In your story, he might be in a plane crash, and you will have to realize beyond a reasonable doubt if he would walk over people to save himself, or make a heroic effort to rescue the trapped toddler in 12C.

If you want to write a novel, it is essential to understand your character as well as you do your best friend, father, lover, spouse, alter ego.

How do you do that?

How did you come to know your wife, boss, mother, college roommate, sister, doorman, stockbroker, father-in-law, house painter? Make a list of things that influenced your judgment. Have you been swayed more by what these people say or do? How much credence do you pay to other people's opinions or reactions to them? When you listen to one of them speak, do you translate what she says into what you think she means? Write down why you do that. Write down the most revealing thing you have ever seen anyone do.

Say at his wedding, when the minister asked your college roommate if he took Shelly to be his lawfully wedded wife, he hesitated so long the guests, the bride, the parents, and the preacher panicked. Was it one incident in a pattern showing he had doubts about Shelly, or simply another example of how this guy never could make up his mind about anything— what classes to take, what to order for lunch?

Your friend has spoiled her child, indulging her every whim. Why? Has she done it because she hasn't the self-confidence to think her daughter would love her if she were a strict parent? Is she compensating for the stern way she was raised? Is this a cowardly pattern that has allowed most people to dominate her?

These exercises are meant to help you organize the skills you have been using all your life to understand people. They will serve you well as a writer.

EXERCISES

- ∞ Name things that reveal someone's taste.
- ∞ List things that show somebody's values.
- ∞ How or when is an individual most apt to show her weaknesses, strengths?

- ➤ What gives you clues about a person's self-confidence?
- ➤ What indicates someone's sense of entitlement?
- ➤ How do you judge presence?
- ➤ Make a list of possessions and property that are character-revealing.
- ➤ What do a person's friends expose about him?
- ➤ What does somebody's home disclose?
- ➤ Name things you can understand about someone by learning how she feels about her family background.
- ➤ How do you discover if a person is intelligent?
- ➤ What indicates obsessive behavior?
- ➤ What does a person's laugh tell you?
- ➤ What do manners disclose?
- ➤ What aspects of someone's physical appearance are character-revealing?
- ➤ What clues does political party loyalty give you about someone?
- ➤ To understand someone, is it important to know her religious persuasion or lack of?
- ➤ How does a person show stinginess?
- ➤ What do you learn from looking at an individual's bookshelves?
- ➤ How could the good causes someone serves be character-revealing?
- ➤ What do you learn by observing the way people treat those who serve them?
- ➤ What type of individuals indulge themselves with massages, manicures, pedicures, facials, make-overs, expensive hair stylists, costly cosmetics?

You will develop your character the way you have come to know your friends, family, enemies, and colleagues: by his actions, thoughts, conversation, tastes, values, dilemmas, conflicts, choices, fears, fetishes, shames; by the way he solves problems, the way other people respond to him. But first you will want to find a character you like, or who interests you enough to spend a year with him on a small sailboat. If you find the right character, she will write your novel for you, at least according to Tennessee Williams, who says in *Where I Live:*

> My characters make my plays . . . they take spirit and body in my mind, nothing they say or do is arbitrary or invented. They build the play around themselves like spiders weaving their web, sea creatures making their shell. I live with them for a year and a half or two years and know them far better than I know myself, but still they must have that quality of life which is shadowy. Was Blanche DuBois a liar? She told many lies in *Streetcar* and yet at heart she was truthful.

When fortune is friendly, your character helps you to know yourself, as Blanche made Williams realize the price he had paid for being attracted to handsome, animalistic brutes.

WORDS THAT MIGHT GIVE YOU IDEAS

cheat	cub	charmer
sucker	sneak	saint
savage	squealer	urchin
plebeian	hack	mama's boy
coward	pet	taskmaster
thinker	patsy	poor sport
hustler	ninny	show-off
has-been	wannabe	quack
hotshot	snob	noble savage
entrepreneur	four-flusher	contender
sinner	eccentric	loudmouth
patrician	hillbilly	outsider
daddy's girl	wheeler-dealer	pushover
trooper	soul sister	spoilsport
autocrat	sob sister	heartbreaker

FINDING A CHARACTER

Novelist Alison Lurie says people read fiction to widen their social circle, to make new friends effortlessly, receive their confidences, and enter their worlds.

Create a character from a frame of mind and a setting you

can understand. Certainly not effortlessly, but you will make a friend, widen your social circle too.

Many beginners erroneously believe they must have experienced it to write it. Emily Brontë wrote *Wuthering Heights*, one of literature's most dramatic love stories, having never been kissed. As far as anyone knows, Stephen King has killed neither man nor animal. You don't have to be a serial killer to write a murder mystery, but some prudence is advised. Research can provide job descriptions, details for the setting and plot. Finding the soul, the motives, and the subtleties of how a character's mind works is up to you.

When a controversy arose over Simon & Schuster's refusal to publish Bret Easton Ellis's *American Psycho* (later published by Random House), *Vanity Fair* magazine asked Norman Mailer if the novel were worthy. Mailer said for a novel to be art, we should know something after reading it we didn't know before. He argued that a murderer must have an inner life for the reader to comprehend him. Mailer feels the reader never gets as close to Ellis's murderer's motives as to his elegant meals or clothes. We never know what drives him, feel no pity for him, because, displaying no fight between good and evil, he is soulless. Ellis doesn't convince us he *understands the inner logic of violence.*

Create a character whose viewpoint you can comprehend. If the Hackensack senior prom, in your cousin's hand-me-down gown, is the closest you've come to a cotillion, creating the sensibilities of a protagonist who attended boarding school, summered in the south of France, and was kidnapped before she came out at The Plaza Hotel for her debutante season could be a hopeless task.

However, you don't have to have smashed your nose scrimmaging with the Bears to write about the dreams and defeats of a defensive end. If your couch has been on the fifty-yard line every Monday night for a dozen years, you probably know the moves and could come to grips with his motives—the inner logic of what makes him run.

Write about what you know and love, want to find out, or have some hope of coming to understand. If you failed geometry and calculus, don't make your protagonist a mathematician. You won't get his jokes. However, if, in a second, you would accept a draft to run for the Senate, delayed your vacation so as not to miss the political convention's keynote speech, and understand the party's platform better than your mayor does, looking through a political character's glasses might be more fun than running for office.

The following exercises are not trivial pursuit. You will be writing to meet a character to call your own, the one who will drive your novel.

E X E R C I S E S

- ❧ Your character's most prized personal possession is _____ _____.

- ❧ His favorite color is _____.
- ❧ Her favorite holiday is _____.
- ❧ The best vacation he ever had was _____ _____.

- ❧ The person she loves most is _____.
- ❧ The friend he respects most is _____.
- ❧ Her greatest fear is _____.
- ❧ What people like best about him is _____ _____.

- ❧ The cruelest thing she ever did was _____ _____.

- ❧ He most regrets _____.
- ❧ She makes plans, or is as spontaneous as a Chicago wind.
- ❧ His fantasy is to _____.
- ❧ Her recurring dream is about _____.
- ❧ The most damaging thing that ever happened to him was _____ _____.

- ❧ The conviction she would go to the wall for is _____ _____.

- ❧ His favorite book is _____.
- ❧ Her favorite relative is _____.
- ❧ He uses the telephone for _____.
- ❧ In her savings account she has $ _____.
- ❧ If he had the choice between going to a Woody Allen movie or to the opera, he would _____.

- Your character is on an expense account; she goes to _____ _____ and orders _____.
- He brags about _____.
- To her, liberal/conservative is a dirty word.
- _____ embarrass him.
- She is afraid people will find out _____.
- He lives in a house, hotel, house trailer, apartment, shanty, van, on a farm, under the bridge, in the governor's mansion, at the shore.
- Her closest brush with death was _____.
- His most treasured memory is _____.
- What she most dislikes about her appearance is _____ _____.
- The talent he would most like to have is _____ _____.
- In her family, she was the firstborn, middle child, baby, only daughter, or _____.
- He is married, single, divorced, widowered.
- Her birthday is _____ , under the astrological sign _____.
- He has _____ children, or hopes to have _____.
- For a pet, she has _____.
- His greatest extravagance is _____.
- She will lie when _____.
- The only thing he ever stole was _____.
- The thing she does secretly is _____.
- He is a Catholic, Baptist, Presbyterian, Episcopalian, Jew, Unitarian, Muslim, Fundamentalist, born-again Christian, Jehovah's Witness, agnostic, atheist.
- If she went to a concert of her choice, the music would be classical, folk, rock, country Western, New Wave, _____.
- He drinks beer, wine, hard liquor, bottled water, juice, soda pop, herbal tea, cappuccino, black coffee.
- She considers _____ the most overrated virtue.

- He considers _____ his greatest achieve-ment.

- Her ancestors came to this country from _____
_____.

- When he is angry, he _____.

- When she is lonely, she _____.

- His idea of perfect happiness is _____.

- The historical figure she most identifies with is _____
_____.

- The living person he most despises is _____
_____.

- The living person she most admires is _____
_____.

- His laugh is:

derisive	*charming*	*cagey*
contagious	*cynical*	*embarrassing*
musical	*loud*	

- Her voice:

sounds like a chime	*is controlled*
is cool and cultured	*is trained, like a singer's/radio*
reflects her origins	*announcer's*
plays at a low volume	*grates, booms, soothes*
is actressy and artificial	

- Create an incident where your character says, or someone says to him, "Your luck seems to have run out."

- Your character would stay in the worst room in the best hotel or in one more appropriate to his circumstances.

- For Christmas, your character always _____
_____.

- How does your character feel about spotted owls, whales, the ozone layer, animal rights, AIDS, ADC, WICK, the ACLU, PACs, police brutality, the defense budget, politically correct prose?

- "In my life _____ moves as slowly as Sunday afternoon," your character says, or someone says to her.

- Show or tell a privilege your character has given himself.

- Create a scene explaining why your character says, or someone says to him, "No one gets bored with hope."

- It has often been said if you need to believe something badly enough, you do. Write a scene in which your character or someone he meets proves it.

- A customs official detains your character because _____.

- " _____ and that night she dined alone."

- Write about a time when your character feels either anger or fear so intense he can't function, or he acts irrationally or inhumanely.

- Develop a scene in which, even though your character is smiling, the edges of her mouth have a tight, overused look.

- Write about a mysterious attendee at a funeral whom your character sees or hears about.

- Write about a loopy moment your character experiences in a serious day.

- Write about how your character behaves on a night when he gets caught in a dreadful storm.

- Picture a closet belonging to a woman living alone. A perfectly starched and ironed man's shirt hangs on a padded hanger. His monogram appears discreetly on the cuff. You know for five years the woman has ritualistically washed and ironed the unworn shirt. Tell why the shirt is there from the viewpoint of the woman, the owner of the shirt, a relative, a cleaning lady. One of these people will be your character or the person who tells him the story.

Eric, the overworked lawyer, doesn't have much time to write, but he finds out a lot about his character when doing exercises in class. He wrote the above closet exercise from the viewpoint of his character, a man feeling trapped by the possessiveness of a new woman in his life. In the middle of the night he finds his shoes in her dishwasher, his pants in the broom closet. As he scurries to the door, the last line is, "The hell with the shirt. . . ." Until he did the exercise, the writer hadn't realized his character wasn't a bachelor, but divorced from a clinging woman.

So many writers have the former mistress or the murderer turn up at a funeral, you will want to try for the unexpected.

Doing the "Your luck seems to have run out" exercise offers an opportunity to work on tone (serious, cynical, funny, playful) and language. If you have found the right words to create the incident, a character can say the sentence sincerely, cynically, cruelly, crudely, but you won't have to include the adverb to tell your reader how to feel. He'll get it.

Tuck the information you've accumulated into your notebook to be used later. Her worst fear might turn out to be the conflict in her story, or his being the only boy in a family of girls could affect his relationship with all of the women in your novel.

Write about a character who intrigues you. It is okay to like him, but don't overlook his warts.

Another tip from Tennessee Williams, who created characters who shone like diamonds and had as many flaws:

> People are humble and frightened and guilty at heart, all of us, no matter how desperately we may try to appear otherwise. We have very little conviction of our essential decency and consequently we are more interested in characters who share our hidden shames and fears. We want plays about us to say, "I understand you. You and I are brothers; the deal is rigged, but let's face and fight it together." It's not the essential dignity, but the essential ambiguity of man that I think needs to be stated.

WORDS THAT MIGHT WORK FOR YOU

stalker	bumpkin	fidgety
slacker	curmudgeon	fluttery
squealer	cutup	cranky
schlemiel	rogue	arrogant
philistine	elitist	goofy
pariah	strutter	flighty
hepcat	winsome	bonny
deviant	daffy	garrulous
bad seed	pigheaded	brusque
quibbler	prissy	laconic
brash	petulant	cute

nincompoop	preppy	self-pitying
androgynous	bogus	pushy
fop	cheap	slick
busybody	elegant	

NAMING YOUR CHARACTER

Kafka and Beckett might have had the ability to create an ambiguous man as nameless as the Unknown Soldier, but most of us have to know how our characters sign their checks.

This is an important moment, second only to christening your child.

Try to imagine Sophie Smith riding a streetcar named Desire to Elysium Fields. Picture a man named Hubert uttering "To be or not to be," or Hamlet loving a woman named Candy. Try saying "Amber" and not thinking "forever," or "Heidi" without seeing goats. However, if you can't think of anything as wondrous as Ishmael, Queequeg, and Ahab, don't despair. Charlotte Brontë did all right with a woman named Jane, and Joseph Conrad made us remember a man called Jim.

The myth about America being a classless society? Would it were true, but names create an impression not only about personality, but also about class and rank. Take Elizabeth, a name of queens. A grown woman who still allows herself to be called Betsy probably won't run IBM, but the one who insists upon being called Elizabeth, even by her lover, might. In a reader's mind, Betty and Bess most likely don't live on the same side of the tracks with Liz and Beth.

I can't help but wonder if the lives of Eleanor Roosevelt, Queen Victoria, and J. Edgar Hoover would have been different if they had been called Ellie, Vickie, and Eddie, respectively.

A horse named Dobbin will never prance like the one called Prince.

Think of the people you know who have appropriate or inappropriate names.

Names often depict the times and the people who chose them. You don't have to check the courthouse records to know a woman named Sunshine or Blue Bell was born in the sixties, while many boys with flower-child mothers can be thankful Bobby Kennedy and Bob Dylan weren't named Hilbert.

Names can also reflect regions of birth. You can gamble on Lady Bird Johnson's never having been asked if she were born in Boston, and on Henry Cabot Lodge's never having been mistaken for a Texan any more than George Herbert Walker Bush was.

You might be able to use how your character was given his name or nickname and the rewards or punishment it provided him. Spunky, Perky, Gay, Merry, Trippy (for the Third) could be hard to live up to on a raw Monday morning.

My cousin named Donna, who was married to Dick, named her children Donald, Derald, Diane, Dwayne, and Dawn. She thought all of the *D*'s looked nice on Christmas cards. I thought those kids who were seldom called by the right names at family reunions might grow up to have identity crises. Don't give your characters similar problems. A reader will have a devil of a time keeping straight a Maggie, Margie, and Minnie in the same story.

You can name your characters anything you wish, of course. Finding the unexpected keeps both editors and readers turning the pages, as long as they believe. Credibility is the only rule. You can cast against type, name an aristocrat Tillie, the chairman of a corporation Jackie, nickname a President Spanky, but people will expect a motive to be revealed, however subtle.

E X E R C I S E S

- ∞ WHAT IF she named her son for a former boyfriend, and her husband didn't know until _____?

- ∞ WHAT IF all your character's life he had been saddled with a rich bachelor uncle's name, on the promise of being his only heir, but in his eighties, the uncle _____ _____ and changed his will?

- ∞ WHAT IF your character moved to a new town and gave herself a new name?

- ∞ WHAT IF your character were snooping around and found his birth certificate had been signed by a mother's name he didn't recognize and the father was listed as "Unknown"?

ᕲ WHAT IF his wife, Mary, insisted upon calling their newborn daughter Mary Junior?

ᕲ WHAT IF the day before the wedding she announced she wouldn't be using his name?

ᕲ WHAT IF his boss called him honey?

ᕲ WHAT IF your character's father named her, his fifth daughter, Stevie?

ᕲ WHAT IF he had grown up having his dad call him dummy or his mother call him baby?

ᕲ WHAT IF for five years he had called her Miss _____ , and then one day, he _____ _____?

ᕲ WHAT IF he gave her a phony name, and the next day she walked into his office?

ᕲ WHAT IF his brother had his father's, grandfather's, and great-grandfather's name?

ᕲ WHAT IF she had a name she couldn't live up to?

ᕲ WHAT IF his name and reputation had preceded him?

ᕲ WHAT IF she had been given a name she outgrew as fast as her first snowsuit?

ᕲ WHAT IF another, not-so-nice guy had his name too?

ᕲ WHAT IF she convinces everyone to call her _____ _____ except her father, who insists upon calling her _____?

ᕲ WHAT IF William Creed Harcourt Blake IV brought home his fiancé, Sweet Georgia Brown, nicknamed Sweetie?

ᕲ WHAT IF your character calls her father Dad, Daddy, Pater, Pop, Popo, Pa, Papa, or, behind his back, "my old man"?

WHAT IF THE CHARACTER IS YOU?

Someone wise said writing is all cross-referencing between our lives and our imaginations.

All novelists draw from their own backgrounds, values, impressions, adventures, but if the character is enough like yourself for you to be sued for plagiarizing your own life, you'll have problems to overcome.

Unfortunately, no matter how interesting your experiences have been, they haven't been structured like a story with a beginning, a middle, and an end. A novel is fueled by conflict (trouble). If you're too close to the story, being honest about the cause can be difficult. Analyzing the effect can be painful at least, sometimes impossible.

When Ronald Reagan was President, his daughter wrote a thinly disguised autobiographical novel. Randall Short, a *New York Times* reviewer, spotlighted the problem:

> In a book so transparently dedicated to letting people know what she thinks Nancy Reagan has done to her, it comes off as a self-dramatizing trick to paste false names on otherwise obvious subjects. (This roman is not à clef but à de verre.) Such a fundamental misstep calls everything else about the book into question . . . Patty Davis has fallen prey to a kind of self-justifying fiction that taints even undisputed facts.

However, Pulitzer Prize winner Jane Smiley says that for many first novelists, it is precisely the desire to settle scores, or to write through anger toward acceptance, that provides the energy for the work. In a favorable review of Sandra Tyler's *Blue Glass*, Smiley said though Tyler relates to the protagonist, her real interest is how the characters relate to one another. Unlike Davis's self-justification, Tyler's larger interest saves the novel from the insularity of many first novels, asserting the uniqueness of these characters and the broader significance of their conflicts.

Start by determining why you want to write an autobiographical tale. If it's for revenge—"I'll show that S.O.B. what he lost when he walked out on me/fired me/chose the other person"—it would probably be more appropriate to talk to a shrink. If you want to make it turn out right this time—you get the girl, the job, the recognition—you could end up with one of those trashy escapist books no one takes seriously—not the way life is, but the way we wish it were. Writing about life exactly as you lived it limits your imagination. Such an exercise could give you insight into how much talent you have for deceiving yourself. The tendency is to glamorize. You are more apt to censor, distort, and protest too much.

If you want to write about loss, for example, a wiser choice would be to create a character who is a composite of your experience and many others'. A writer's most powerful stimulant is WHAT IF . . . what if I had lived in Alaska . . . what if I had been ten years older . . . what if "this character" had five children . . . what if she went to clown school, ran for office, started a dude ranch. . . ?

A memoir by definition is self-referential, but need not be self-absorbed. The daunting process of rediscovering the past requires an outward as well as an inward view.

In another life, Terre had a successful television career. Fortunately, rather than creating a glamorous persona to brag about her own triumphs, in the workshop she created Grace Lord, a mosaic of many ingenues, put her on a turf Terre knows well, and dug into Grace's character.

Hemingway, one of the more autobiographical writers, used his life as material but transformed it into a symbol of the human condition, arousing universal pity and fear. When he was wounded in the war, he wrote *The Sun Also Rises*, built on the thesis, war wounds us all, literally or figuratively. As an old man worried about his talent drying up, he created a fisherman trying to hook one last big one. The last big one was *The Old Man and the Sea*.

E X E R C I S E S

- The period of my life I want to delve into is _____
  _____, because _____.
- The friction was caused by _____.
- What changed was _____.
- My blind spot could be _____.
- If the story is recognized as mine, the gain could be _____.
- If the story is recognized as mine, the danger is _____.
- If I changed the character's profession, _____.
- If I wrote from the viewpoint of the opposite sex, _____.
- If I moved the action to another state, city, country, _____.

- ☞ If I looked at how an older/younger character would have handled the situation, _____.
- ☞ The story could be more interesting if the character were _____ or had done _____.
- ☞ An interesting character to tell this story might be _____.

At night Rona plays the lead in the Broadway musical *Miss Saigon*. In the workshop, drawing on her knowledge of creating illusion, she writes a fantasy novel about a princess named Russia.

DESCRIBING YOUR CHARACTER'S APPEARANCE

If your whale is going to be white, tell the reader in the beginning, or she will paint him with dirty dishwater. Edgar Allan Poe had such high regard for his readers he often consciously left out details, assuming they would imagine something more vivid, more grotesque, more pleasing to them than he could supply. But when a character's appearance or physical vitality has significance, like Lenny's size and strength in *Of Mice and Men*, let it be known right away. If you don't say immediately, she is six feet seven inches tall or he has a hump on his back, forget it. These facts won't wait until Chapter Seven. Your character's face and physique will already exist in the minds of the young woman reading your story on the subway and the guy in the recliner in Peoria. They will feel cheated or tricked.

Don't even think about starting your story until you have a mental picture of your character so clear an artist could draw her picture from your description and you could order her clothes in the right size, down to knowing if she would need control-top panty hose. Why waste the energy when few of the details will end up in the story? You want to create a character so real your reader could recognize him at a school board meeting or on the D.C. shuttle and remember her as long as he has the first girl he ever kissed. The way people look affects what they think, say, do, and others' reactions to them. Fat men break chairs at dinner parties. Short women have difficulty with tall podiums and finding their kids in a crowd. Some people think "dumb blonde" is a compound word. Kids laugh at men with big ears and little hats.

Even though it is necessary for you to know what your character looks like, in some stories physical appearance has little if any consequence. What goes on inside someone's head usually makes a better story than his hat size. Raskolnikov's contemplating breaking the laws of God and man and the consequences of his action are what we remember from *Crime and Punishment*. I had to go back to find that Dostoyevsky describes him as having delicate features. The author doesn't seem to take his looks very seriously either. In an offhand sentence, he says, "By the way, he was remarkably handsome, with wonderful dark eyes and light-brown hair, about average in height and slim and graceful." He devotes almost six hundred pages to the significance of Raskolnikov's philosophy.

Teenagers who spend half their time in front of the bathroom mirror and the other half sending their stories to *Seventeen* magazine go for physical appearance, especially the color, length, and style of hair, flawless complexions, and FIGURES. Beginning writers usually spend more time describing the ubiquitous "blond hair and blue eyes" than necessary, because every other aspect of the human face and form is more difficult to capture and the perfect human spirit is not advertised in slick magazines.

If how your character looks is important, studying photographs by professional photographers such as Richard Avedon, Annie Liebowitz, or Diane Orbis and pictures in magazines while you practice portraying your characters' features can help you find the language. How close one's eyes sit to the nose can be descriptive, as can hairlines.

Observing people in public places is something writers do. Parks, theater lobbies, and especially baseball games are good spots. People sit funny on bleachers. Try to scrutinize without staring. Seeing like a writer should not lead to your being assaulted or arrested.

With a compelling story in progress, I was riding the Fifth Avenue bus one afternoon around three o'clock (in the viewpoint of my character, of course, as a disciplined method actor-writer always does). At a stop near a private school, with much fanfare, a group of twelve- or thirteen-year-old girls boarded, showing skinny, coltish legs below uniform skirts with plackets twisted every which way. I know I came out of my seat, maybe even said something aloud—perhaps "Eureka!"—because the woman sitting next to me pulled so far away she almost fell into the aisle.

There she was! Right here on the M104. My character's daughter, who was breaking her mother's heart because she didn't fit in. The face I had been looking for was the shy one with straight bangs and the long braid, black as beans . . . belonging to the only girl who still had her shirttail tucked in. Flipping a shock of permed hay, the loud one with the vocal cords of a bingo caller, obviously the leader of the pack, was embarrassing her to death. "Oh, forget her," the noisy one was saying faster than I could write. "Samantha won't do it. She'll go straight home and practice her dumb ole cel-loooo like she always does."

Oh, but she would, her mother, barely resisting the urge to shake the bingo caller, was muttering in my ear. *Give her the slightest sign you want to include her . . . she'll do it. . . . Samantha, giggle, honey, or push your knee socks down . . . see how theirs flop around their ankles. . . .*

With Samantha's mother's interior monologue still running, we got off at the next stop, dashing home to the computer without even bothering to put the notebook back in my pocket.

I included Samantha's braid but spent more words on her tidy appearance, which revealed character. Even though a novel gives you more room to roam around in than a short story, wasting words still doesn't work. Squandering seventy-five words to explain your character's height is being a spend-thrift, unless it's necessary for the reader to know he could unscrew a light bulb without having a stepladder handy, or he has always been an awkward kisser because he has a penchant for short women.

There are probably more blue-eyed blondes and tall, broad-shouldered men trapped in unpublished manuscripts than the latest census takers found answering real doorbells. If you want your character to stand out (not all characters should; think of Camus's stranger), give him something un-usual or unique. I was once married to a big man with a head as round as a basketball, who liked to be remembered. Even before I became a writer, I convinced him to shave his head. Once on a cruise ship, a stranger, watching my husband tower over a crowd gathered around to hear a story he was telling, said to me, "I'll never forget that man. He looks like an old baby."

The literary character's portrait etched in my mind from here to eternity is Eustacia Vye—Queen of Night—whose passion and instincts "make a model goddess" but . . . "not quite a model woman." Although Hardy eventually describes her "pagan eyes, full of nocturnal mysteries" and hair "a whole winter did not contain darkness enough to form its shadow," what I remember is a tall figure wrapped in a cloak whipped by a wind off Egdon Heath, silhouetted in the night by the light of red coals from a dying bonfire, defined by her "conspicuous loneliness, her utter absence of fear." Like the poet he also was, Hardy managed to use physical attributes, clothes, and environment to liberate a character from words to life.

Picturing your character in his environment helps to bring him into focus. Think of Jay Gatsby's house.

James Gatz, a young man who was poor, bootlegged some whiskey, bought a pile of monogrammed shirts, and became Jay Gatsby, making himself up from scratch, which is pretty funny when you think Fitzgerald made him up in the first place; but nevertheless, it's a literary device that often works well. In *The Sun Also Rises*, Lady Brett Ashley, who wanted to be one of the guys, bobbed her hair, wore a man's hat, and bellied up to the bar with the best of them. Hemingway didn't approve of her getting herself up in this unisex garb, but readers paid him no mind and have admired her forever. Gatsby's shirts and Brett's hat give a clearer picture of them than their hair color or height.

DESCRIBING CHARACTERS THROUGH ALLUSIONS

Saying your character is a James Bond look-alike is a shortcut into a blind alley. Ian Fleming will be remembered for creating the fearless Bond. You might not be published at all. I know you can show me thirty-three examples in print of allusions to Marilyn Monroe's body or Willie Loman's slump, but that wasn't the reason the stories were published. Trust me. Describe your own character so a reader could recognize him in a movie queue, and maybe the next generation of writers will be alluding to him.

SHOWING, NOT TELLING, PHYSICAL APPEARANCE

Assume your reader is sensitive and intelligent; therefore, it will not be necessary for you to make judgments for her. If you give her the pertinent details, she will decide if someone looks and acts like a champ or a chump.

If you really want to write a novel, make a sign to hang over your desk: SHOW, DON'T TELL! Show what? Everything—actually, almost everything. When you come to a spot where it makes sense to tell the reader it's three o'clock in the morning, rather than creating a wall and a clock, you'll know. Showing actions, feelings, and even physical appearance is more effective, especially to our television generation of readers.

You are introducing a character who is dangerously overweight and whose size will have consequences in the story. You could say, "Suellen was grossly fat," telling the reader not only what she looks like, but also how to feel about her. Or you could say, "Trying to find a booth set far enough back from the table for her comfort, Suellen thought how wonderful it would have been to live in the Renaissance, when artists liked their models hefty."

Often you will be able to accomplish a dual purpose by having another character give the description. For example, "He couldn't take his eyes off the new chick with the bikini figure sent over from the typing pool. How long had it been since Helen wet her lips enticingly like that when she spoke to him? Of course, his wife never had this kid's ripe, pouty lips and wouldn't have painted them a sexy fuschia color if she had."

Writing from the inside and the outside adds an emotional aspect to a character portrait. The reader not only gets an impression of the woman from the typing pool, a sense of her age and manner, but also forms an attitude about the person observing her.

When your character opens the nursery door to find his wife sitting cross-legged in the playpen rolling a ball to the baby, and he says, "How appropriate," rather than, "Isn't that cute?" you know not only she is short, but the marriage might be too.

To start creating the picture of your character, try the following:

E X E R C I S E S

- ∽ My character's most outstanding feature is _____ _____. Its significance in the development of the story or in revealing his character is _____.
- ∽ Her being attractive/ugly is necessary because _____,
- ∽ He wears a size _____ shoe. I will/will not include the size in my story.
- ∽ She wears an Almost A, 38–D, 34–B bra. The reader will/will not need to know the cup size.
- ∽ In repose, you notice the laugh lines/the frown tracks on your character's face.
- ∽ His hands look like a catcher's mitt, or his fingers are so long and slender he could model rings, he bites his nails or has a knockout manicure, he uses his hands with the skill of a conductor or they seem to get in his way, as if they belonged some other place or to someone else, or _____.
- ∽ He has a nose no one would notice; one no one can miss, etched with red-and-blue broken blood vessels; one that had obviously been bobbed; wide, flaring nostrils showing hair that needs to be clipped; or _____.
- ∽ Her lips were full, dry, chapped, pale, pouty, tight, turning down at the corners, shaped like a candy heart, or _____.
- ∽ Describe anything about his appearance which causes people to make the wrong assumption about his personality, like deep-set dark eyes that make this pushover look like a villain in a melodrama.
- ∽ Describe something she wears to disguise a flaw.
- ∽ Being proudest of his _____, he dressed to show it to his best advantage.

- ✤ She looked like her _____, but wished she had inherited _____.

- ✤ His siblings were jealous of his _____, or he was jealous of their _____.

- ✤ If she had had the body or the face, she would have been _____, or because she had the shape and features, she had chosen to _____ _____.

- ✤ Put your character in a setting like her office, his workshop, on a skateboard, at a dance, in a place that helps the reader to see him more clearly.

- ✤ Dress your character in something that emphasizes his body, face, good looks, homeliness, averageness.

- ✤ Your character tries to create the impression of being _____ by doing/saying/not telling _____.

- ✤ Your character looks like _____. Describe that person's appearance without using the name of the well-known person or character.

- ✤ Write from the inside and the outside to have another character reveal her impression of your character.

- ✤ If your character were tapped to play an extra in a movie, the role would be a _____.

- ✤ Your character tends to remind people of spring, summer, fall, or winter. Explain.

- ✤ Describe your character's:

ears	elbows	rib cage
teeth	legs	posture
ankles	biceps	self-image
public face	eyebrows	

WORDS THAT MIGHT WORK

lush	repulsive	squinty
elfin	girlish	frumpy
knobby	dowdy	elongated
gamine	stunning	plain
creepy	sensual	bulbous

DRESSING YOUR CHARACTER
FOR SUCCESS

Think of the last time you went shopping with someone. What did his purchases tell you about him? Is he decisive or hesitant? Does he dress to please himself, others, or to create the image of his profession or job? Are clothes a vice or a necessity? Is he extravagant, tight, a show-off, practical? Does he follow trends? Does he prefer bright, cool, or dark colors? What did his taste reveal about his background? If you went shopping with your character, how would you answer these questions? Could you use the material to develop your plot or reveal character?

Attire has been known to bring out hidden sides of people's nature. A wimp struts in a uniform; a woman—proud in a business suit—cowers in a bathing suit; put her in a clown suit and she becomes one; he uses his umbrella like a swagger stick; he tipped his hat only when wearing a skimmer; short skirts freed her flirtatious nature; even his new clothes looked as if they had been wadded up; he wore a tux as if it were his birthday suit.

Choice of clothes can be revealing. I've always been convinced men who wear boxer shorts, even if they have cute tushes, vote Republican, buy blue-chip stocks, and play polo.

Garments are much easier to write about than jealousy or pride, but we don't remember Othello and Oedipus because of their togas. When you dress a character, the questions are:

- ∞ What do I gain by describing what she is wearing?
- ∞ Does the reader need to know?
- ∞ Am I indulging myself in a personal interest that does nothing for my story, or does her dress with red poppies, jacket that's too tight, jeans from the army surplus store, feather in her hat, pin in her bra strap, jade bracelet, have consequences or significance?

To get a lot of good out of the clothes your characters wear, think of ways to make them mean more than is immediately apparent. Her all-red wardrobe is bound to cause repercussions. Keep in mind the shabby bathrobe he won't give up could lead to divorce if she learns not only did Sally give it to him in Venice, but he has never stopped loving Sally for a minute. If he continues to buy her preppy clothes even after she explains she prefers frills, something more is at stake than Brooks Brothers being close to his office.

In Fitzgerald's imagination, rich girls were always bored and always wore white dresses. Literary tradition has it that bad guys wear black and FBI agents wear dark blue suits, sometimes with brown shoes. Women educated in Catholic girls' schools wear white gloves and slips, even in the summer. In the Midwest our purses and our shoes always match. Women from old money wear cloth coats even if they live in a cold climate. The nouveaux riches wear ermine, sable, and mink even if they live in Miami. You can use traditions, mores, old wives' tales, clichés to create irony, show the past, or for contrast, but even when choosing costumes for your characters, it's best to develop your own style.

EXERCISES

- One piece of clothing that helps to define your character is a ratty bathrobe, a French beret, a cape with a red satin lining, spike heels, or _____.

- When your character wants to make a good impression, he wears _____.

- To a fancy charity ball, your character would wear _____ _____.

- She is most comfortable when she wears _____ _____.

- He buys most of his clothes at _____.

- If she could afford it, she would buy a _____ _____.

- To work he wears _____, but in his imagination he wears _____.

- She wears _____ to create the impression she is _____.

- When he buys clothes, he always considers what _____ _____ will think.

- When she was growing up, she wore _____

_____, but for her children, she buys _____.

∽ If he were a designer, he would create a piece of clothing that _____.

∽ She would like to wear _____, but can't because _____.

∽ His favorite tie is from his school, has a painted hula dancer, advertises his company's product, is red as a tulip, costs as much as the weekly grocery budget for a family of four healthy eaters, or _____.

∽ Words that might lead to something:

slingbacks	fun fur	stained
skimmer	ascot	garish
corset	teddy	gossamer
cross-dressing	bow tie	funky
man-tailored	synthetic	flashy
white bucks	tacky	vulgar
morning coat	crumpled	yellowed

The murder victim in John's mystery was found in a lavender nightgown. Her name was Addie, but everyone in the workshop always referred to her as the woman in the lavender gown.

PROPS FOR YOUR CHARACTER

On the stage, dramatists give characters props like cherry trees to chop down, whips to crack, plates of food to throw, dead sea gulls to drive them crazy, Yorick's skull to push them into reveries, Hedda's pistols to fiddle with. Props that make a difference have symbolic and realistic value. Hedda's pistols (one would never call them guns, even for the sake of variety) not only give her a weapon to use for her suicide, but they provide a psychological grounding for the character's behavior.

Novelists provide props for their characters too, but always for a purpose. You never have a character open a book, pet the dog, unless there is a reason. In my workshops, most of the participants' mean, evil, ugly people light cigarettes in every paragraph. We had to discuss the writers' intentions. Those who could defend their character's action could keep the cigarette, but those whose well-intended—if thinly disguised—aim was to persuade me to stop smoking need to find a better prop and a more effective line of argument.

Writers who call themselves Mommy or Daddy when talking to their cats will probably object to thinking of animals as props, but they can be effective. Politicians understand animal appeal. People who can't tell you anything about his New Deal remember FDR's little dog, Fala. Richard Nixon's "Checkers" speech is as famous as Watergate. No struggling writer will ever forget how many copies Barbara Bush's *Millie's Book* sold. And in the first year of the Clinton Administration, Chelsea's cat, Socks, reportedly received more letters than Ann Landers.

Jack London and Herman Melville, two of many who have written moving stories involving animals, would also object to my categorizing creatures as props. In defense, I do not mean to imply a guinea pig or a canary will have no more personality than your character's red velvet smoking jacket or Queequeg's pipe.

Actually, as I work on this manuscript in a rented house on the Maine seacoast, I am at war with Brutus—a raucous, strong-willed sea gull with nasty personal habits and a red spot under his beak that makes him look as if he puts his lipstick on upside down. He is already in my notebook and will surely work his way into a story and demand a more important role than that of a mere prop. Personality? Brutus is more obsessive than Ahab.

The first evening, after placing a snack tray on the deck, I was returning for the wine when he swooped in, greedily grabbing his share. I shooed and shrieked, but not only did his shrill backtalk drown me out, he also stared me down with his beady pink eyes. That bird knows I thought *Jonathan Livingston Seagull* was a perfectly silly book, I assumed, until I learned Brutus has a backstory. The owner of the house feeds him. This is his turf. He brutishly defends it from other gulls and belligerently demands I serve him. Since Brutus's voice would raise the dead and silence any muse, I tried earplugs; he was louder. I pulled the drapes on the window; he scolded me from his perch on the door. . . . It's not who wins, but how we play the game. So what's a few crackers? Besides, I have a deadline. And he could be material.

I've known cars as bullheaded as Brutus. In modern America, automobiles—or in some areas, pickups—have replaced the cowboy's horse and, to many of us, have as much significance. Think about cars you've owned that have personalities as distinct as your kids. Maybe you can weave one into your story. In nightmares, I still sometimes swear at a red Volkswagen bug, a convertible named Fritz I once drove. On a blustery winter morning in Chicago, that was the stubbornest, orneriest critter ever to roll off an assembly line.

Hester Prynne's scarlet letter takes first place for symbolic props, followed closely by Miss Havisham's wedding dress, Huck and Jim's raft, Tom's picket fence, Finny's tree in *A Separate Peace,* and Holden Caulfield's hunting cap.

Don't develop a case of writer's block if you don't have a symbolic prop on the tip of your tongue. Not all novels have obvious symbols. Many writers who have developed wonderful ones claim they were unconscious creations. Faulkner swore his bear was just a bear, but coming from a writer who admits to having built *The Sound and the Fury* out of an image of Caddie's muddy drawers, it's hard to believe.

EXERCISES

- ↪ Describe what your character wears in the lapel of his jacket and why he fiddles with it in tight situations.

- ↪ Explain something worthless your character wouldn't sell for a fortune.

- ↪ Show something significant your character always carries in her wallet.

- ↪ On the wall of his office he displays _____ _____.

- ↪ She always wears a yellowed ivory bracelet or _____ _____. Show its symbolic significance, or use it as a clue to _____.

- ↪ When he travels, the first thing he packs is _____ _____.

- ↪ For a pet, your character has tropical fish, a snake called Satan, a horse named Hamlet, twenty-three cats, a pit bull, or _____.

- Sitting on her desk is _____.

- Your character drives a jeep, a pickup truck, a BMW, a Harley Davidson hog, a Rolls-Royce, his dad's hand-me-down, a dune buggy, a restored 1957 T-bird, his girlfriend's rusty wreck, the Pontiac he received for high school graduation, or _____.

- The only sticker he ever put on his bumper said _____ _____.

- On weekends she wears a T-shirt that says _____ _____.

- No matter where he lives, he has to have a _____ _____.

- All that is left from her failed marriage is _____ _____.

- How might the following be props in your story?

  a hearing aid
  a pearl necklace
  a ring on a chain
  a scrapbook
  a photograph
  a rock collection
  a pig cookie jar
  a filofax
  an unused airline ticket
  a uniform
  a sidesaddle
  a lace handkerchief
  a record collection
  a dead houseplant
  a business card
  a will
  a uniform stored in mothballs
  a red lace negligee still in the box

  a safe
  a set of keys
  an oil lamp
  a signed baseball
  a motorcycle
  a pressed flower
  a high school yearbook
  a rusty red wagon
  a gravestone
  a rubber hose
  a bronzed shoe
  a pince-nez
  a fortune from a cookie
  a bundle of letters
  a receipt
  a teddy bear
  a bank lockbox
  a handmade Christmas tree ornament

Wayne used his character's attachment to a marijuana pipe to reinforce his alienation from the other citizens in a small, conservative Southern town.

DETERMINING YOUR CHARACTER'S MOTIVATION

A novelist can get away with almost anything in a novel except not understanding her character's incentive. Motivation, the justification for the character's action, holds the story together as the keystone in a building. A writer is obligated to present a convincing and impelling cause for action.

You might not know why you get up in the morning, but before you start your story, if you don't know why your character does, you might as well stay in bed.

This won't be so hard. You have had lots of practice. Remember when you figured out why your son cut his hair in a Mohawk, your shrink's personal relationships are a mess, your boss enjoys reprimanding people publicly?

The chief difference between puerile fiction and great works of imaginative power rests on motivation. A plot-driven, action-filled story can be content to unfold a series of thrilling, unnatural episodes, exciting in themselves, but growing out of no inherent purpose other than the author's desire to excite his reader. You know the type—a seduction in every chapter, shoot-outs, chases, fires, stabbings, collapsing buildings, sinking boats, wolves crawling out of sheep's clothing.

A motivated deed, however, is action justified by the makeup of the character doing the act, making the decision. Shakespeare's Falstaff is a wit, not a hero, who runs from the battlefield and the scene of a robbery.

Readers want to know not only what a character does, but why she does it. A cynic says no young, aristocratic Venetian woman would elope against her father's wishes to marry an older, dark-skinned Moor. Shakespeare says Desdemona would, but he goes to great pains to develop her motive— being charmed and enchanted by Othello's exotic past.

Some things you never get over. The impetus for our actions often is something carried over from childhood, simply modified to fit adult behavior.

Once, a man I knew well—well enough to know he planned business trips when we argued or when things weren't going well with his staff—unintentionally explained his behavior. Reminiscing, he told me that as a rowdy little boy, he used to cause family rows when he wrecked toys from his intimidating grandmother. A clever optimist even as a child, to avoid everyone's wrath he would put the broken toys in the closet, close the door, go out to play and hope they would get well. After hearing the story, I used to say when he called from the road, "I'm still in the closet, but I didn't get well."

Usually, motivation consists of a combination of psychological traits and external events. If it is worked out satisfactorily, it leaves the reader with a recognition of those emotive and circumstantial forces that make the action inevitable, like Midas's greed.

E X E R C I S E S

- ᴄ WHAT IF your character wanted revenge?
- ᴄ WHAT IF your character feared he would follow in his father's footsteps?
- ᴄ What if your character had always felt she was responsible for her brother's death, her parents' divorce, her husband's failure, her children's rebellion?
- ᴄ WHAT IF your character, a single mother who had been artificially inseminated, had a son who at age ten demanded to meet his father?
- ᴄ WHAT IF your character couldn't face the reality of his life?
- ᴄ WHAT IF your character were a moral coward?
- ᴄ WHAT IF your character had always felt left out?
- ᴄ WHAT IF your character had always felt deprived?
- ᴄ WHAT IF your character's religious education had marked her?
- ᴄ WHAT IF being extremely poor/rich had marked him?
- ᴄ WHAT IF your character blamed her father?
- ᴄ WHAT IF your character were pathologically shy?

⮞ WHAT IF your character had not been able to get over the loss?

⮞ WHAT IF your character couldn't handle the success of his father/brother/friend/enemy/wife/child?

⮞ WHAT IF your character were ashamed?

⮞ WHAT IF your character were lazy?

⮞ WHAT IF your character had a stubborn streak?

⮞ WHAT IF your character had been spoiled by doting parents?

⮞ WHAT IF your character could no longer live up to past deeds?

⮞ WHAT IF your character couldn't handle authority?

⮞ WHAT IF fear ruled your character's life?

⮞ WHAT IF the need for attention ruled your character's life?

⮞ WHAT IF your character couldn't handle conflict?

⮞ WHAT IF your character convinced herself her deceptions were benign?

⮞ WHAT IF, as an adult, he punished every woman in his life for his mother not having loved him?

⮞ WHAT IF, in her vision, no man was as tall as her father?

⮞ WHAT IF your character were as romantic as Don Quixote?

⮞ WHAT IF your character were as loyal as Sancho Panza?

⮞ WHAT IF your character had an incurable need to please?

⮞ WHAT IF he stayed only because of the division-of-property law?

⮞ Your character feels justified when he _____ _____.

⮞ Your character panics when she _____.

⮞ Your character does something outrageous when _____ _____.

Her workshop colleagues were horrified when Maria's Kitty went to work for Blackstone, one of the city's most powerful and corrupt politicians. "Even nice girls can be fascinated by the wild side," she replied.

MINOR CHARACTERS

Now that you've done the hard part, coming to grips with what force drives your character, interesting and necessary minor characters should be a piece of cake.

Selecting to tell Sam's, or Sally's, or Sinbad's story, you have also made plot and structure decisions you might not yet realize. By choosing a main character, you have built a frame around your novel encompassing only the people and events that have an impact on your protagonist at a certain period in her life. You will create many other characters who also have full, interesting, or strange lives, but you will be able to include only those aspects of their existence that relate to your character's story.

Let's say it's Sam's story. He is a brain surgeon who lives in a town house in Washington, D.C. The neighbors in his complex could be the movers and shakers at the State Department or on The Hill, but unless their lives and work have some bearing on Sam's life or reveal something about his character, forget it. This is Sam's story. His therapist might be a bungee jumper, have a fifteen-year-old daughter who made the Olympic swimming team, and be having an affair with a librarian afraid of heights and water, but unless this information has some consequence in Sam's life, put it in your notebook, not in your novel. Write about the therapist next time. This is Sam's story.

Mark Twain really had one story to tell. It was about the two sides of his nature. The first time he told it in *The Adventures of Tom Sawyer,* from the romantic, imaginative Tom's point of view. In that story Tom had a friend, Huck Finn, who was a minor character in the tale. The next time Twain told it better, with the uncivilized but sensitive Huck as the main character and Tom having only a slight and pretty silly role in the story.

Jim, Huck's companion on the raft, is a minor character, but for Twain to show how Huck's natural goodness wins a battle over the social mores of the time, he had to create a fully developed character the reader would root for. We see Jim's strength, his loyalty, his fears, his affection for Huck; we hear about his family, listen in on his dreams, but the tale always belongs to Huck. What we learn about the sympathetic character, Jim, is included for the purpose of exposing the corrupting values and beliefs of the time, so when Huck makes the decision not to return the slave to his owner, the reader cheers for Huck's noble decision. We see the events from Huck's point of view, understand how his conscience moves him to make decisions and often to feel guilty. Jim's story on the raft hasn't been told yet.

Talk about audacity, first prize goes to Tom Stoppard for *Rosenkrantz & Guildenstern Are Dead,* a wonderful literary spoof in which Hamlet is a minor character.

Alice, a classical scholar, joined the writers' group when Lucian, an ancient Syrian sophist who had been the topic of her dissertation, refused to move out of her mind. In her novel, she chose to have him tell his tale in the first person, as Huck had done. In a short time she realized arrogant Lucian needed a foil. When she created foxy Xenophone, an educated Roman slave, the other writers applauded, but Alice had as much difficulty keeping this interesting character in his place as Lucian did. Maybe Xenophone's story will be the sequel.

In your novel, you will need essential minor characters like Jim and Xenophone, but you will also create waiters, redcaps, truck drivers who might appear only once with little consequence other than carrying a bag or serving your character runny eggs. Whether you describe their physical appearance, clothing, actions, will be determined not only by your plot, but more by your style. There is no rule. Henry James's servants were sticks with no faces, but Dickens's florid style rendered him incapable of creating even the least significant character who didn't come into focus by wearing something weird or having a hook nose or a tic you couldn't miss.

The operative question when developing minor characters is "What is their relationship to my main character and what significance does their alliance have in this story?"

Doing a few of the following exercises might help you discover minor characters who assist in revealing your character's nature or in telling his story.

E X E R C I S E S

☞ The most important person in my character's life is _____
_____.

☞ My character's worst enemy is _____.

∽ The members of her family she pays attention to are _____
  _____.

∽ The person my character would most like to forget is _____
  _____.

∽ The person who has a bad influence on my character is ____
  _____.

∽ The most impressive person my character ever met was ____
  _____.

∽ My character will always be loyal to _____
  because_____.

∽ _____ has been my character's best
  friend since _____.

∽ Even though he is older, my character feels close to _____
  _____ because _____.

∽ _____'s youth made her even more appealing because _____.

∽ My character feels sorry for or guilty about _____
  because _____.

∽ WHAT IF your character meets someone who makes her feel
  like a backup singer?

∽ WHAT IF your character meets someone who makes the ma-
  cabre mundane?

∽ WHAT IF your character meets someone wearing an ankle-
  length mink or trench coat? The coat accidentally falls
  open _____.

∽ WHAT IF your character meets someone who has smelly feet?

∽ WHAT IF no one ever lived up to _____
  or at least the memory of her?

∽ WHAT IF your character finds herself involved with a man
  who makes her blush because he blushes at nothing?

∽ WHAT IF your character meets someone from society's un-
  derbelly so poor, so ignorant, he has fallen out of the main-
  stream and operates by his own rules?

∽ WHAT IF your character meets someone who appears so
  glamorous, so accomplished, she feels the person has to be
  a fake?

∽ WHAT IF your character meets someone so damaged by his
  life he has lost hope?

- WHAT IF your character meets someone who says, "Don't send me long-stemmed American Beauties. I'd rather have a rosebush"?
- WHAT IF your character meets someone who interrupts conversations to correct everyone's grammar?
- WHAT IF your character has an affair with his boss?
- WHAT IF the nerd she wouldn't marry in college makes it big?
- WHAT IF the sycophant in his office snows his boss?
- Write about someone your character meets who is a "corker."
- Create a character who has a goiter on her neck.
- Your character collides with a comet—a romantic woman, a power-hungry colleague, an appealing child who won't let go . . .
- Write about someone your character meets who makes all the wrong choices for the right reasons, sometimes desperately.
- Write about someone your character meets who is half angel, half hectoring witch.
- Write about someone your character knows who is so ambitious he could have been arrested for indecent exposure.
- Your character meets someone from the social stratum that has always raised its children to assume their own superiority—and also to mask that assumption at all times. Create a scene to show it.
- Your character meets someone whose boyhood mean streak has matured into an appetite for success in his career or business.
- Your character meets someone who hides her pain behind a cynical shield.
- Your character meets someone he once knew who never amounted to much, and listens as he tries to explain why.
- Your character is influenced in a profound manner by a radio or TV host she has never met.
- Your character gets sucked into the whirlpool life of someone who lives on the edge.
- Your character meets someone who needs attention so badly she couldn't stand to be left out of an epidemic.
- Your character meets someone who suffered from griefs, not grievances.

∞ Your character meets someone who reminds him of a friendly beach ball.

∞ Your character meets someone who says she needs dreaming room. Set the stage.

∞ Your character meets someone who has "strutting splendidly" honed to an effective deception of how she actually feels about herself.

∞ Your character "sort of" falls for someone who is more rat than romantic hero.

∞ The evening he met a street woman who called herself Hope because she couldn't remember her name, he _____ _____.

∞ After twenty years as a faithful husband, your character meets someone who makes him feel like a poetic superman who could fly right over his responsibility and guilty conscience.

∞ After the children are in college, your character meets someone who makes her feel as if Lady Chatterly has found her lover.

∞ Your character meets someone who has a personal grace that allows him always to seem to know what to say to people to charm, make them feel better, or cause them to adore him.

∞ Your character meets someone whose voice is actressy, a tad artificial, a voice that seeks to charm. She sprinkles her conversation liberally with "divine," "darling," "charming," "I'm all aglow."

∞ Your character meets a real live country Western singer. He has the boots, the hat, the string tie, the tight pants, the cocky stance . . . everything except the horse and a distinctive voice.

∞ Design a scene which ends or begins with your character saying, "I guess he/she wasn't such a bad egg."

∞ Show the dogged loyalist who disgusted everyone, sometimes even her hero, whom she would crawl on her belly to serve.

∞ Without making a judgment, describe the physical characteristics of an important minor character in your story.

In the workshop, minor characters like Maria's uncle Nellie, yesterday's Mafia boss, or Steve's Ryan, a detective burned

out by too many uncivilized crimes, have backstories waiting
to be told.

STOCK OR STEREOTYPED CHARACTERS

If the urge to create a tight-lipped sheriff who lets his gun do
the talking overcomes you, take a walk. Remember, John
Wayne is dead. Other ghosts of stories past to exorcise are
Hemingway's stoic heroes who have all been wounded in
some heroic way in territories that lose their purity if a
woman invades. You will also need more than a monocle to
prop up a proper Englishman, more than a pint of stout to
create a souse of an Irishman, more than a lisp and a limp
wrist to portray a gay.

Scholars speculate that Shakespeare worked fast, like
writing *Macbeth* in three weeks. One reason might have been
his reliance on stock characters, types which recur repeat-
edly. He did a brilliant job with Falstaff as the braggart soldier, but personally, I could have managed with fewer
heroines disguised as handsome young men and clever servants who outwit the stupid gull.

Those of you who grew up on television, where all conflicts
must be resolved in an hour, will have the most difficult time
obliterating stock or stereotyped characters from your subconscious. Hookers with hearts of gold, rich men whose
money has made them miserable, the valiant poor who have
found God and will search for a cat in a blizzard, gum-chew-
ing typists who are really smarter than their bosses, are
shortcuts that don't lead to a fully realized character.

Political correctness has had an impact on conventional
characters, especially on stock minority roles. Uncle Tom is
apt to have an M.B.A.; a tough woman solves the crime; the
good teacher speaks Spanish.

I am not suggesting you absolutely cannot use prototypes.
What better Horatio Alger type than Gatsby? Emma Bovary,
Lady Chatterly, and Kate Chopin's Edna Pontellier certainly
added an interesting twist to Sleeping Beauty. You can build
a memorable character from an archetype if your re-creation
is individualized. Billy Budd, Huck Finn, and Holden Caulfield were cut from the same innocent pattern.

A great deal of criticism exists pointing to characters such
as the Fatal Woman, the Ruthless Male Hero, the Devil, and

God as archetypal patterns that recur because they express universal aspects of man's unconscious mind. Jung, a psychologist, describes archetypes as primordial images formed by repeated experiences in the lives of our ancestors, inherited in the "collective unconscious" of the human race.

The collective American unconscious, reinforced by male writers from Twain to Hemingway, has created a horde of good/good girls and the good/bad boys who have all the fun. In *Gleanings,* my young adult novel with one of the worst titles ever published, I reversed the types. Pepper, the good/bad girl, played the Tom Sawyer role. Frankie, the good/good boy, played Becky Thatcher; he tried to make her behave herself. In *The Robber Bride,* Margaret Atwood takes the role reversal a step farther. Her Zenia is a bad/bad girl.

If you borrow from the cultural attic, give your Devil characteristics that set him apart from the others. Metaphorical tails and eyes that glow as red as Christmas tree bulbs have already been done.

E X E R C I S E S

- ↝ Physically describe a cowboy who neither alludes to nor brings to mind John Wayne, Clint Eastwood, or Shane.

- ↝ What job-related conflicts would today's cowboy face that didn't exist for his ancestors?

- ↝ What would motivate a man or woman in the nineties to work on a ranch?

- ↝ Create a scene between your character and a cop on the beat that works against type.

- ↝ Introduce a minority character whose skin color, shape of eyes, or religion is included in a way that identifies but is not judgmental, defensive, sentimental, or self-conscious.

- ↝ Create a wealthy person who is defined by her traits of character rather than by things money can buy.

- ↝ What is today's melodrama? Who impersonates the victim, the villain, and the savior? What role does the lawyer play?

- ↝ Describe a young gang member who is a Robin Hood type without sentimentalizing him. How could you show his charm him a hungry grandmother at death's door?

ᗧ Introduce a credible May/December romance in which the older person is female and not as rich as cream.

ᗧ What contemporary theme would call for Peter Pan revisited?

Steve spends too many days in juvenile court to think kids accused of violent crimes are all shaped in the same mold. He gives an Oedipal twist to his story about a young black man accused of murder.

ANTAGONIST

If your character is pitted against an important opponent, you have an antagonist, someone who will be an important and well-developed minor character. Father/son stories often cast one as the antagonist—he who stands directly opposed to the main character. In a business environment, the protagonist will often have a rival who stands between her and her goal. When a love story is a triangle, the third person can be an antagonist.

The conflict in your story does not have to arise from trouble between your hero and another person, but when it does, the dissension will help to structure the novel. Anxiety about who is going to win, what is going to happen to the character we like, creates suspense. If what does happen violates the expectations we have formed, as O. Henry was known to do, it is a surprise. The interplay of suspense and surprise is a prime source for the magnetic power of a plot, but the most effective surprise is that which has been thoroughly grounded in what has gone before. E. M. Forster said even though the reader made the wrong inference from the given facts, if the shock of the unexpected is followed by the feeling of "Oh, that's all right," it's a sign that all's well with the plot.

If an antagonist sets up a scheme which depends for its success on the ignorance of your character, the plan creates intrigue. A special kind of suspense called dramatic irony arises when the reader sees the oncoming disaster but the character does not. Readers love dramatic irony because it makes them feel smart. Of course, you can allow the reader to be in on the antagonist's thoughts and feelings about the intrigue only if you're telling the story from the omniscient point of view, which lets you move from one character to another. (In another chapter we will explore viewpoint options in greater detail.) If you narrate your story from the main character's viewpoint, the intrigue need not be lost, however. You can create situations where he misses clues, or his naïveté, fear, or blinding loyalty tricks him.

Think of the times a smitten friend has introduced you to Mister Right, who you recognize immediately is as wrong as ants at a picnic. He is after her money, her apartment, her job—anything but her heart. Or analyze the situation in your office where everyone sees the writing on the wall except the person who is being set up by someone as clever as Iago. Most of us have known people who avoid looking at the signs of impending disasters. Use the indicators they miss to create dramatic irony in your story.

Antagonists can be mean as snakes or as well intentioned as missionaries, but you have to show their motivation as well as you do your protagonist's. Greed, revenge, fear drive people to do awful things, but good people can cause pain for reasons they can justify. Look at Annawake Fourkiller, the Native American lawyer in Barbara Kingsolver's *Pigs in Heaven*, who has reason to believe children shouldn't be adopted out of the tribe. The unfortunate fate of Annawake's twin brother doesn't ease the pain for Taylor, the white mother whose adopted daughter Annawake is trying to reclaim for the Cherokee Nation.

However, some of the most effective antagonists—from ghosts to Godot—never appear. Their presence is felt through the words and deeds of the people they trouble. Dead people, like Daphne Du Maurier's Rebecca, the late first wife, have also been effective antagonists, especially in love stories.

E X E R C I S E S

- ∞ WHAT IF a younger man, brought into your character's organization, created a new layer of reporting order between your character and his former boss?

- ∞ WHAT IF the reporter sincerely believed your character was responsible for something that was not his fault?

- ∽ WHAT IF your character discovered her sister was not only trying to turn her fiancé against her, but was also professing to be in love with him?
- ∽ WHAT IF her first husband were out to get him any way he could?
- ∽ WHAT IF your character had alienated a high-ranking official in the IRS?
- ∽ WHAT IF your character discovered a member of his campaign staff had been secretly working for the opposition all along?
- ∽ WHAT IF her rival were her mother?
- ∽ WHAT IF the super in his building hated him for unknown reasons?
- ∽ WHAT IF her brother announced he was going to marry the woman who had been her foe since kindergarten?
- ∽ WHAT IF the competition lay between him and his best friend?
- ∽ WHAT IF she learned the rumors were being spread by her roommate?
- ∽ WHAT IF their families were old enemies?
- ∽ WHAT IF she discovered she had a stalker?
- ∽ WHAT IF his child hated her?
- ∽ WHAT IF her secretary hated him?
- ∽ WHAT IF his competitor were handicapped?
- ∽ WHAT IF her enemy were a member of a minority?
- ∽ WHAT IF his enemy were gaudy rich?
- ∽ WHAT IF jealousy were the motive?
- ∽ WHAT IF she alienated the professor?
- ∽ WHAT IF his enemy were a cop?
- ∽ WHAT IF his enemy were a zealot?
- ∽ WHAT IF, legally, his antagonist had grounds?
- ∽ Describe the physical appearance of your character's antagonist.
- ∽ What is your character's antagonist's name?
- ∽ Write a scene showing your character and her antagonist in the same meeting.

Wayne's antagonist is Barnett—his character's brutal redneck father who has been dead for twenty years but never lets up on his son. But Marc's character's adversary doesn't have a face. The young yuppie lawyer wrestles with the values of the greedy eighties that shaped his generation's expectations. Both characters have enemies to fight that create suspense and tension in the story.

CHAPTER 8

Finding Your Character's Story

At this point you have a character you would recognize in the dark. You know his name, his family background, his tastes, his values, his politics, his friends, his enemies, his flaws, his obsessions, his bank balance, as well as how many cavities he has in his teeth, when and to whom he lost his virginity, if he sends Mother's Day cards, if he is a leader or a loser, if he has life insurance and a cemetery plot, if he puts sugar in his tea, and if he is afraid of the dark or the water.

There is much more to uncover, but you will find it by seeing how he reacts in tight corners, on rainy Sunday afternoons, when his team loses, when she wins . . .

Developing his story is the next step.

STORY VERSUS PLOT

In the beginning I said stories happen only to people who can tell them. Everybody has a story, if you or someone would just write it. A fully loaded DC-10 carries enough tales for volumes of a modern version of *The Decameron.* The passengers only wait for their Boccaccio, as anyone knows who identifies herself as a writer to a talkative seatmate. The man not so "far from the madding crowd's ignoble strife" who makes his home on a warm grate, the sullen checker at the grocery store, the boy who tosses your paper—usually in the bushes—the kindergarten teacher who still hugs your son after he pours his milk on the class's ant colony, live lives that make novels when you sift through their experience and analyze their character to determine why their lives have taken the turns they have.

E. M. Forster put the difference between story and plot most succinctly in *Aspects of the Novel* when he said that the king died and then the queen died is a *story* (a narrative of events arranged in their time sequence), but the king died and then the queen died of a broken heart is a *plot*. In a story we ask, "And then what happened?" In a plot we ask, "Why did that happen?"

Although for clarity we are discussing character, story, plot, language, setting, .etc., in separate chapters in this book, you create your character's world as a whole. Action, thoughts, dialogue, incidents, are influenced by where the story takes place as well as who is involved. Having grown up on four hundred acres in the Midwest, in a house for which we didn't have a key, I have a story different from my friend who spent her entire life in apartments on the Upper West Side of New York City.

If you were born in Cleveland, people in Georgia talk funny and folks in Louisiana eat things, without even cooking them, that look too weird to put in your mouth.

When you find a character who intrigues you, she comes with a story . . . once upon a time, there was a . . . (all tales begin like that in some way or other). The next question is "And then what happened?" . . . but what if she made a bad choice, lost her lease, got pregnant, told a lie, met a charming loser, found a purse; or there were a heat wave . . . ?

Think of your story like a tangled ball of yarn you are going to unwind. On the very first page, even if you are only describing your character or the setting, you want to raise questions, suspicions, and expectations so the reader turns the page wanting to know what has already happened, what is going to happen, and how it will unfold. You might write, "If she had bothered to look, Mary Margaret would have seen her face had shriveled up like an old monkey's, but it had been a long time since this once proud woman had taken a good look in the mirror." What has taken her pride? What has aged her? Has she done something she can't face?

I've discussed novel ideas with dozens and dozens of writers, many who had not yet put a word on paper, but I've never found anyone who had a character who didn't appear in her imagination with at least a semblance of a story. Not all of them are scoops, nor are they meant to be. Jackie Collins's and Judith Krantz's characters—whose names I no longer remember—inherit fortunes, become movie stars, meet Prince Charming, but it's Mary McGarry Morris's Martha Horgan, a tad slow and never like the other girls in *A Dangerous Woman,* whom I'll never forget. My mind is an apartment house for characters who won't move out, like Cormac McCarthy's sixteen-year-old John Grady Cole, who rides over the Mexican border in *All the Pretty Horses,* breaks promises but never lies to the horses; or Alice Hoffman's free-spirited Nora in *Seventh Heaven,* who has a great knack for selling Tupperware to the husbands in her new neighborhood.

Your characters, like your friends, carry baggage from the past and dreams for the future. Let's say you want to write about a woman in her thirties. You probably already know she is divorced, supporting her child by working on a tuna boat off Nantucket, or single, trying to make vice president in a thorny bank in Burbank, or raising three kids with her lazy husband who is supposed to be a carpenter in Cincinnati. Don't be spooked if you don't already know everything that happens to her during the year, six weeks, one day of her life you plan to spend with her. Just listen. She'll tell you her story. When she moves into your mind, the problem will be getting her to stop talking. Good characters tend to be like those long-winded people whose telephone calls you dread on a busy day.

Not all writers know why their story has happened until after they've written the first draft. You will be amazed at how much more you learn about your character by writing about him.

When Wayne finished his first draft, even though the people in his group brought champagne to the workshop, he seemed a bit droopy. "I reread several early chapters. They embarrassed me," he said. "I have so much to cut that doesn't do a darned thing for the story . . . in Chapter Three the pacing stopped dead while I preached a sermon rather than advancing my plot. . . ." As others finished, they began to sound like a Greek chorus. Shaking his head in disbelief, Jim said, "The conflict is introduced too late. The first thirty pages have to go. I was just finding my way." "Tell me about it," Heather responded. "I wasted one whole chapter introducing a person who never appears again—someone I now realize my character wouldn't have anything to do with in the first place."

Because we learn about our characters and ourselves as

we write is why so many writers work on a computer. Wayne's problem could have been a time killer and a chore, especially in the summer, if he weren't doing his rewrite on a laptop at the beach, on his Brooklyn roof, or any place he pleased. To do their revisions, Jim went home to Oregon, Heather to Vermont. They packed a disk the size of a slice of cheese.

You come to recognize what goes into and what has to be fixed in your own story, not only by writing it, but by reading other authors' novels from a writer's viewpoint, always asking why an event took place, a character behaved as he did, particular information was included. In a later chapter we will look in more detail at the difference between a character-driven and an action-driven plot, but for now, concentrate on fleshing out your character's story by working on some exercises that could expand your idea. Serendipitously, you might recognize an incident, a situation, an environment that helps to advance your plot, or meet a character who reveals a telling aspect of your protagonist's nature. At least you will have probed deeper into her personality, maybe even her soul.

Just as you know more about your protagonist's character than you will have time and space to show overtly, you will have to pick and choose which people, incidents, and events to include and what and who can be left out of the story. For example, there is a novel in every short story. The author plucked one time period, one dramatic moment, out of someone's life, but that doesn't mean the character didn't live another twenty years, or that before the story opened, he hadn't had other highs and lows in his life.

Since you would bore a reader to death, to say nothing of never finishing your novel, if you began with your character's birth and followed her through to her funeral, you will know much more than you tell. Doing the exercises will begin to help you make the choices.

EXERCISES

√ WHAT IF your character encountered the one person who had always been able to reduce her to rubble?

√ WHAT IF your character observes a pickpocket in action?

- ☞ WHAT IF, after twenty years of marriage, he said, "I never did love you"?
- ☞ WHAT IF someone said to your character, "Look at you. Just look at you."?
- ☞ WHAT IF he got her job?
- ☞ WHAT IF she were left out of the will?
- ☞ WHAT IF he left his daughter out of his will?
- ☞ WHAT IF the dishwasher overflowed or the oven blew up?
- ☞ WHAT IF your character walked into his boss's office, telling himself, "Cowards die many deaths"?
- ☞ WHAT IF she said, "That's emotional blackmail"?
- ☞ WHAT IF he got sick?
- ☞ WHAT IF, on his honeymoon in Bermuda, he sent a girl in Kansas a blue sweater because the sea and sky reminded him of how she always had looked good in blue?
- ☞ WHAT IF she told him she was HIV positive after they had made love?
- ☞ WHAT IF he told her he was gay after the baby was born?
- ☞ WHAT IF she wished she never had to pull into that familiar driveway again?
- ☞ WHAT IF he found someone's wallet? The owner's name, address, and telephone number were prominently displayed. His returning or not returning it complicated his life.
- ☞ WHAT IF, acting out of an excess of optimism, she miscalculated and the situation became messy, funny, sad, heartbreaking?
- ☞ WHAT IF someone who had hurt him said, "Judge not, that ye be not judged"?
- ☞ WHAT IF a letter changed everything?
- ☞ WHAT IF your character met someone from the past? They realized nothing in either of their lives equaled the moments they'd had ten years ago.
- ☞ WHAT IF she sent him a card with a picture of a cowboy but didn't dare sign her name?
- ☞ WHAT IF even he realized he was slipping?
- ☞ WHAT IF, after the divorce and his remarriage, her former

husband called? He said he made a mistake, he was sorry, and he wanted her back.

ᴄᴐ Write about a time when she felt she didn't have a friend in the world.

ᴄᴐ Write about a time when your character would have written about himself using an *i* and it wouldn't have been a typo.

ᴄᴐ Write about a time when she had every reason to hope for the best.

ᴄᴐ Write about a time when he disappointed someone so deeply, things could never be the same.

ᴄᴐ Write about a time when your character threw away her heart as if it were a used bus ticket.

ᴄᴐ Write about a time when a casual remark from a professor changed his life.

ᴄᴐ Your character didn't even realize he was jealous until she _____.

ᴄᴐ At first she didn't think she would mind that included in the baggage he brought from another marriage were four boys aged seven to fourteen, until one day _____ _____.

ᴄᴐ Design a scene in which your character says or thinks all will be forgiven. Nothing will be forgotten.

ᴄᴐ When she opened the front door, a black bear was in her house . . .

ᴄᴐ The moment he tore it into dozens of pieces, he was sorry. Describe the situation and identify "it."

ᴄᴐ The moment she dropped it in the mail, she was sorry.

ᴄᴐ Your character hears only a few bars. He stops and thinks, Jesus, that was our song. . . .

ᴄᴐ He dressed, left the house, but that day he just couldn't force himself to go to work, so he _____.

ᴄᴐ Your character is the type who would lead the band, or the type who tries to maintain a low profile. Create a scene showing this trait.

ᴄᴐ Your character thought the best offense was a strong defense, until she said he'd fouled out for charging her and earned a technical for name-calling. Build the situation.

∽ She didn't even see it coming until _____ _____.

∽ When he won five hundred dollars in the football lottery, he _____.

∽ Her mother said, "I always knew you would _____ _____.

∽ He thought everyone suffered from a "father hunger" and his wasn't any worse than other people's, until _____ _____.

∽ Your character reports high drama or impending disaster from a car phone.

∽ _____ tells your character evil is born from innocence itself, like hers.

∽ _____ had stuck to him all these years like a piece of tar he couldn't scrape off his shoe.

∽ "Don't give me any problems I can't solve," your character says, or someone says to him, and can't understand why his remark is upsetting.

∽ It has often been said if you need to believe something badly enough, you do. Show a scene where your character or someone she meets proves it.

∽ Your character wishes he never had to open the door to his office again.

∽ In the silence of the bathroom, your character smiles at herself in the mirror and says, "(her name), I forgive you."

∽ Your character says, "I don't always show the wisdom of Solomon, but you can count on this . . ."

∽ "When you're childless, other women treat you funny, like you might be weird or a kidnapper or something," your character says.

∽ It started with parking tickets piling up; then he missed a couple of student-loan and insurance payments. Before he knew it, there seemed to be no way out.

∽ Your character receives a notice from the IRS saying her former husband owes an enormous sum in back taxes from a year she signed a joint return. He has disappeared. Therefore, she is responsible.

Chip had written himself and his protagonist into a corner. When his character, a husband and father, accepted that he was gay, Chip realized he had painted such a flawless, unrealistic picture of the wife that the character he intended to be sympathetic didn't have a chance with the reader. He began to take a deeper look at her with the exercise, WHAT IF a letter changed everything? A relative with AIDS announced a visit. The good mother saying "No way" gave Chip an opening to explore her defenses and denial.

PICKING A POINT OF VIEW

One of the most important decisions you have to make about your novel—the choice that will affect every other aspect of your story—will be to pick your storyteller. When you write that first line, who will be saying, "Once upon a time in Peoria, Illinois, a man hopped a freight instead of going to his law office"? His voice could well be what determines the success of your story!

Realizing that actions by themselves are generally of limited interest, Henry James spoke of the need for a "mirroring of consciousness" and gave major attention to choosing the right "reflector." You probably know someone who can turn a walk around the block into a story everyone listens to eagerly. Contrast her with the person who could meet a man from Mars and no one would want to hear the tale, even if he got the alien's calling card. Then there's the person who could find the gloomy aspect of a winning lotto ticket or the chirper who always looks on the sunny side. A narrator's voice, tone, language, pacing, distance, choice of details, intelligence, insight, will make all the difference in your novel.

FIRST-PERSON NARRATOR

A person within the story—the main character, a minor player, or merely a witness—may tell the story after he experienced it, saw it, heard it, and understood it, or any of the above could relate the events as they are happening. In the latter instance, the action is proceeding while the pages are being turned. No matter what his relation to the events, the first-person narrator is the "I" who is telling the story.

Reliability is the major issue. An author may purposely create a naive first-person narrator, like Huck Finn, who does not comprehend the implications of what he is telling. An ingenuous storyteller chosen for a purpose such as contrasting natural innocence to schooled evil or maturity can be effective. Think how differently you and your children tell about an experience you share. Also, we all know adults whose views of events and people are shaped by the narrowness of their own experiences or by their fears and intolerances. You've met the person with a trust fund who thinks people are rich because they are the chosen.

A disingenuous "I" narrator whose intent is to present a subjective view of a situation, or a person who is warped or clever but crazy, as some of Poe's storytellers are, can tell a splendid tale. However, a first-person narrator becomes a bore if the author is the one who doesn't seem to fathom the significance of his storyteller's bias, defensiveness, limitations, or has a superficial understanding of the twists and turns of fate and life itself. That situation most often happens when the narrator is based on a character too close to your own life, or you are writing about someone from a stratum, a lifestyle, or a profession strange to you.

Norma Fox Mazer, a writer from a blue-collar family, tells about giving up on her first story after the first page when, as a teenage first-person narrator, she tried to write about a girl in a boarding school but hadn't a clue to how such a school functioned, how boarding-school girls looked at the world, or how much allowance they received.

If you decide to assume the persona of your character to tell the story from the I-was-there, it is vital for you to understand his environment as well as his personality.

A first-person narrator, sharing his thoughts, feelings, and experiences, has a more intimate relationship with the reader than when the reader is being told by someone else how a character feels or thinks; however, this point of view restricts the writer. After you've chosen a viewpoint, you are locked in. A first-person narrator means you won't be able to probe as deeply into the personalities of other characters because you will always be writing from the outside, what your narrator assumes they are thinking or feeling, never from inside their heads.

Also, you can't write yourself into a corner and switch to another perspective to get out. You can include only what your narrator sees, thinks, or hears. Let's say he is a sergeant in the army. You can't include a conversation his superiors have about him at the officers' club. But there are ways around such a situation. One of his buddies, who is a waiter, could tell him about overhearing the conversation.

Describing the physical appearance or personality of a first-person narrator can also be tricky. She can't say, "I have a gorgeous turned-up nose men want to kiss," unless you want her to be an egotist. But if that nose is important, you can have a man say he would like to kiss her cute turned-up nose.

Also, your first-person narrator can interpret the way he is looking at her so the reader sees a picture. For example, "Maybe wide hips don't turn him off. He sure can't miss mine, or the hammy upper arms I inherited from Dad. But he still looks as if he wouldn't mind paying for me by the pound." Showing your "I" narrator's personality through her actions, like having her buy a $400 blouse when she has $100 in her checking account, will be more effective than having her say she is reckless.

OMNISCIENT NARRATOR

At the other extreme, the author (or her persona) may serve as an all-knowing omniscient narrator, not restricted to time, place, or character, but free to move and to comment at will. This vantage point is analogous to a television camera that can zoom in and out of any of the actors' perspectives. The omniscient narrator can objectively report what is happening to any or all characters. He can interpret any character's appearance, speech, actions, and thoughts, even if the character cannot do so.

Here you have free access to the motivation, thoughts, and feelings of all of your characters, not just those of a single person, as is the case with a first-person viewpoint. But as an omniscient narrator, you would be wise to restrict your insights to two or three important characters. I once read a confusing Louis L'Amour novel told from seventeen viewpoints—one was a horse's and another a bear's.

Herman Melville, in *Billy Budd*, is interested in the conflict between innocence and evil in man's nature and in society as a whole, as Mark Twain had been with Huck, but Melville chose to explore it from an omniscient viewpoint. We know the thoughts and feelings of the evil Claggart, the natural Billy, and the traditional Captain Vere, caught in the middle.

As an omniscient narrator, you can also, speaking in your own voice, introduce information, background—like naval history, as Melville did in *Billy Budd*—to the reader when and where you choose. The omniscient narrator can offer objective observations too, but use common sense. When a scene is intimate or intense and your presence would be intrusive, you should vanish.

Although the omniscient point of view is much less restricting, the reader probably won't become as involved with your characters as he will when he is confined to one person's perspective of this topsy-turvy world.

THIRD-PERSON NARRATOR

Another option is to narrate the story in the third person, but to choose one character as your sentient center, whom you follow throughout the action. This viewpoint restricts the reader to the field of vision and range of knowledge of that character alone, as the first-person narration does, but in the third person the author can comment, as he can't do in the first person.

Point of view is simply who is speaking. When you write, "She opened the door and saw a dead mouse," you—the author—are speaking, contrasted to first-person "I opened the door and saw a dead mouse," where the character is speaking.

MULTIPLE NARRATORS

More writers seem to choose the third-person point of view, but to refresh your memory about other options that have served writers well, you might want to review some of the following: Emily Brontë used two witnesses—Nellie Dean, the housekeeper, and Mr. Lockwood, a tenant—to narrate *Wuthering Heights*. Joseph Conrad often let Marlow, a yarn-spinning sailor, relate stories like *Youth* and *Heart of Darkness* from his memories, observations, and hearsay. Critics have often seen Marlow, Lockwood, and Nellie as unreliable narrators, but Fitzgerald's Nick, who tells *The Great Gatsby*, is usually heralded as the most trustworthy of witness narrators.

In Rosellen Brown's novel *Before and After*, a girl is murdered and seventeen-year-old Jacob Reiser stands accused. Brown tells the story from the Reiser family's point of view, but not from the traditional omniscient viewpoint. She jumps not only from one perspective to another, but also from first to third person, revealing the Reiser family from a multitude of angles, as though you are seeing them in a room with many mirrors.

Lipsha Morrissey, Louise Erdrich's protagonist in *The Bingo Palace*, tell his story in the first person, but Erdrich gives many other characters' viewpoints in chapters narrated in the third person.

YOUTHFUL NARRATORS

Several recent adult novels are told from the viewpoint of young people. A nostalgic voice generally signals an adult story, while a more immediate voice makes a book feel more aimed at a younger reader.

Sam, a teenager, tells Bobbie Ann Mason's *In Country*, a tale about the aftermath of the Vietnam war. Dorothy Allison's first novel, *Bastard out of Carolina*, is narrated from the perspective of a child who is the victim of incest. *Weddings and Wakes*, Alice McDermott's story of an Irish-Catholic family on Long Island, is told through the eyes of the youngest members—two sisters and their brother.

TRICKY NARRATIVE FORMS

Reynolds Price's *Blue Calhoun* is a 373-page letter Blue writes to his young granddaughter. *Even Cowgirls Get the Blues* is told in the second person. Either narrative form is acceptable, but such an awkward way to tell a story, I recommend . . . forgive me, I know this verb doesn't usually need to be qualified, but I *highly* recommend you not try either one in your first novel.

PSYCHIC DISTANCE OF THE NARRATOR

Think of novels you have read where you felt as if you were actually experiencing the emotions and the actions along with the character. If he were lost in a rainstorm, you felt wet; if she had a broken heart, you were bereft; if his secretary nagged, you became impatient; if she experienced danger, you were afraid. In these cases, the reader feels a narrow gap between herself and the events in the story, like, "Hard, sharp rain. Sheets of it blown by the harsh wind, wrapping around her like a blanket of nails. Her icy feet sloshing in soaked shoes, rivulets running down her neck, the kind that can freeze your mind . . ."

Other narrators keep their readers at arm's length: "In a small town in Idaho, a woman stepped out into a rainstorm totally unprepared for the onslaught."

The psychic distance you put between your narrator and reader can vary according to the scene, but the trick is to avoid distracting shifts in which the reader is zoomed in and out for no apparent reason. For example, "Lily despised rain. Scares me to death, if the truth were known, she thought, but of course I'm not about to admit it to any of these busybodies. This elderly woman had experienced many bad storms since she moved to Idaho."

Think of the technique as if you were using a camera. You can view a scene from far away, move in nearer and nearer, until you are shooting a close-up according to the effect you are trying to create. Notice how the following begin remote in time and space, but narrow the span until the distance is nearly nonexistent.

A. One night, on a dark city street, a young woman was accosted by a man armed with a small pistol.

B. Bonnie Burns was frightened when she saw the man appear out of the shadows.

C. Bonnie's throat tightened in terror when she realized the man had a weapon.

D. Oh, God, he's going to kill me, she thought as she felt the gun on her neck.

E. A gun! Cold as an icicle on your neck. It's moving . . . don't panic. You must not panic. Oh, no, God wouldn't let him shoot me in the ear. Not in the ear, Please, not . . .

Edgar Allan Poe believed in short narratives because he said a reader could not sustain the emotional intensity for long periods of time. This was probably true for his readers because of the close, intimate psychic distance he maintained with his audience throughout the story. In his tragedies, Shakespeare interspersed comic relief to give the viewers a break from the pain and suspense.

In anything you write—letters, a memo, reports—you choose a psychic distance which conveys your attitude, intent, and relationship with the person you're addressing. The style and language in a letter which begins with "To whom it may concern" are quite different from one that starts with "Hi, Old Buddy."

When I began to write this book, I decided to address you directly in the first person, as if you were a student in my class or a participant in a workshop. I wanted the psychic distance to be so close it seemed as if I could reach over to point out a missing comma in your story. I could have chosen the more formal style of most textbook writers, like, "Writers have the choice of three major points of view, which are . . ."

Although there are numerous exceptions, novels most often open with the narrator at a greater psychic distance, slowly narrowing the gap, and moving in close for intense scenes.

The following exercises are designed for you to gain experience in thinking about how to focus a scene, as well as to discover which viewpoint comes easiest.

E X E R C I S E S

- ∞ The car of an out-of-control driver jumps the curb, barely missing your character. Write the scene from the driver's point of view (first person) as the incident is taking place.

- ∞ Re-create the scene from your character's point of view, as he tells it a few weeks later.

- ∞ Write the same scene from your character's point of view, but in the third person.

℞ Rewrite the scene from an omniscient viewpoint, including the driver's and other pedestrians' perspectives.

℞ From a first-person viewpoint, have your adult character tell about his first day in school. This will be told in *flashback*, a technique of superimposing the past on the present. Flashbacks work better written in the past perfect—"had been worrying" instead of "was worrying." When you switch back to the present, the verb tense helps with the transition.

℞ From a third-person viewpoint, flash back to your character's first date.

℞ Writing from the omniscient point of view, create a scene at a cocktail party your character attends.

℞ Your character meets an attractive person of the opposite sex. Write the scene in the first person.

℞ Describe from a third-person viewpoint your character's impression of his father-in-law's behavior at a Thanksgiving dinner.

℞ Use an omniscient point of view to describe the meal.

℞ Your character is frightened. Write it from the first-person viewpoint with little psychic distance. Write it from third-person points of view, widening the psychic distance.

℞ Create a scene where your character is in a staff meeting. Show his colleagues' feelings about him, using the three different viewpoints.

℞ Daisy Chowder is struck by a hit-and-run driver. Write the scene in three versions, each time narrowing the psychic distance.

℞ Write what might be the opening paragraph of your story from the three different points of view.

℞ Explain where your character was born and raised from his point of view. Give the same information from a narrator's viewpoint.

℞ Writing from your character's first-person perspective, give the reader a picture of her appearance from the way she interprets how someone is looking at her.

℞ Describe your character's physical appearance from a narrator's perspective.

℞ Have your character give the reader a picture of his physical appearance through dialogue and his thoughts (first person) as he meets someone important for the first time.

↪ Create a conversation in which your character reveals her relative age and education without actually saying, "I am thirty-five years old and did not finish high school."

Home on The Ranch is Marsha' story, but Jessy's challenge is to express her viewpoint from three perspectives: when she is in a normal frame of mind, manic, or depressed.

TONE

Parents, teachers, supervisors, often reprimand their charges by saying, "I don't like your tone." Perhaps the person in question has said something cynical, sarcastic, egotistical, humble, or has responded humorously to a serious situation. His language and manner of speaking have expressed his attitude toward the person to whom he is speaking, toward the situation, or toward himself.

Think of the times you have been interviewing someone for a job and were either immediately impressed or turned off by his attitude toward himself, you, the world in general. Just as you quickly decided you could not endure spending eight hours each day in his dour, cynical, naive presence, a reader (or an agent or editor) will make an equally quick decision about spending three hundred pages with your narrator.

Keep in mind, people's first impression of your story will come from the same criteria you used to judge the potential employee—who is telling the story, and what her attitude (tone) is. They will decide, maybe on the first page, certainly in the first chapter, if she is cranky, judgmental, funny, intelligent, and if they want to spend several hours listening to her voice.

As you read the following possible first lines in which the main character is expressing his opinion about his father, visualize the type of person speaking:

"My old man, he ain't much to brag about. Mule-stupid, is what I'd call him."

"Without my meritorious father's love and guidance, I would never have made it through the rigors of academic life."

"Me? I'm just a plunker. But if you want to see someone

make these ivories dance, watch my dad. I'd be grateful for a quarter of that guy's talent."

"Dad reminds me of a duck waddling along, afraid his pants are going to fall down. Squawks like one too."

The story each of the characters tells will be shaped by his attitude. Tone is also used to create the mood of the work. A writer's tone can be formal, informal, intimate, solemn, somber, sarcastic, awed, playful, serious, ironic, condescending, sympathetic, contemptuous, or any of many other possible choices.

To set the tone of a scene, an actor on the stage can use facial expressions—a frown or a grin—or actions like slapping his leg or covering his face—but your characters must rely on language—what they say, the words you use to show how they say it, how others respond. Language sets the tone.

By now you probably know your character well enough to understand how self-confident he is, what kind of expectations he has, what kind of outlook he has on the world. However, if you're still exploring your protagonist's or other major character's opinions, try some of the warm-up exercises.

EXERCISES

- ∽ Describe August, having your character use a sarcastic tone.

- ∽ Describe December, having your character use a somber tone.

- ∽ Describe June, having your character use a humorous tone.

- ∽ Describe September, having your character use a whimsical tone.

- ∽ Write a scene in which your character meets someone who awes her.

- ∽ Re-create the scene above, showing your character's ironic attitude (his implied attitude is the opposite of what he says) toward the person he meets.

- ∽ Design a scene in which your character speaks in a formal way to express her feelings about putting her family responsibilities first.

- ∽ Rewrite the scene, having your character speak in a humorous, informal way about the same subject.

✐ Write dialogue that expresses your character's cynical opinion about life after death.

✐ Write dialogue to express your character's serious concerns about the afterlife.

✐ Write sentences showing your character's stating someone has died, using the following verbs to change the tone of each sentence: "departed," "croaked," "passed on," "deceased."

✐ Your character's daughter has a boyfriend. List four words her father might use to describe the young man that would convey different attitudes.

✐ A lost child wanders into the park carrying a white kitty with a blue bow around its neck. Write the incident from the viewpoint of someone whose tone is as sentimental as a Hallmark card. Rewrite the scene from the perspective of someone whose tone is as sarcastic as W. C. Fields's, even about kids and kitties. Write it again with a humorous tone.

✐ Your character's boss calls him into her office to explain the yearly raise he will be receiving. Write the scene from the viewpoint of a sycophant, a hotshot, and a worried man.

✐ Describe the shuttle taking off from a space station in the voice of a woman with a Ph.D. in physics. Describe the same scene in the voice of a five-year-old whose father is on board.

✐ An officer has a black teenage boy spread-eagled across his cruiser as he searches him for a weapon he thinks he used to rob a newsstand. Write the scene in the tone of a bigot. Rewrite the scene in the tone of the boy's mother. Create the same incident in the tone of a member of the ACLU.

✐ Describe a party in the tone of a pretentious snob.

✐ Describe the same party in the tone of an ingenuous young woman.

✐ Describe the party in the tone of someone who is bored.

✐ Describe the party in the tone of a comic.

✐ Describe the party in the tone of a crook who plans to rob the guests.

Jeremy's Solomon Wise's attitude toward himself causes him the most heartache. When he thinks about life after death, he imagines himself as ashes in an urn no one would want. He sees the urn being overturned and himself ending up being swept into a vacuum-cleaner bag.

LANGUAGE

If that perverse imp who can turn anyone into a doubting Thomas has begun to do his dirty work on you, shoo the pest away. No, you are not Jane Austen or William Faulkner, nor were you meant to be. Copies of anything from writing styles to Chanel bags hold little worth. You have a unique voice. Value lies in developing it in your distinct style and tone.

You have a story and a character eagerly saying, "Wait until you hear this." You have a lifetime of experience, and you've been thinking like a writer. Observing, listening, really seeing. Language expresses thought, and you have the words too. If you know the alphabet from A to Z, what do you have to worry about? With those twenty-six letters, you can make every word that Shakespeare ever wrote and more. Many fine novels have been written by people who did not have a clue to what pneumoconiosis meant or how to spell it or any other polysyllabic word. Usually the right word, the one that makes all the difference, is as common and comfortable as your favorite pair of jeans. Recently, Alice brought tears to some other writers' eyes when she had a child put his head on an *unfriendly* shoulder.

Painting a picture of his character's deadbeat father, Jim had his character remember Dad insisted the family eat *mushy* tomatoes. "Ripe," even "overripe," would not have created the same degree of disgust.

Julie put her protagonist, a professional woman, in the kitchen, where, preparing for her husband's return after a trip, she chooses the menu based on what pots are clean. She thinks, I'm sloppy but creative, as she uses the contents of the refrigerator to make soup out of a bottle of beer, a ham bone, stale pumpernickel, a cauliflower—slightly wilted—and a can of good chicken stock. By the time she has chopped, sliced, simmered her way through the soup, dropped butter on her suit, and goes to put on a sweater her husband gave her and jeans, but leaves her earrings on, she has created far more than a sense of place. Thirty minutes later, when Julie's character drops her usual ironic tone, looks in the mirror, and thinks, I must really love that guy, the reader is convinced.

Julie's scene is set for romance, but predictability makes boring stories. The character's husband ate on the plane. He has troubles. She fixes a tray for herself, following him first into the living room and then to the bedroom, where he covers his face with a pillow. She thinks he would probably like to be alone, but she is tired of schlepping the tray all over the house, and besides, she's hungry. The soup wasn't bad.

In most cases, when it's mealtime in your story, you'll take care of it in three words: "She fixed dinner." (Unfortunately, if *he* fixed dinner, it's probably character development and will need explanation.) The description of Julie's dinner preparations required a page, but she had a purpose. Use your words as frugally as you budget your money. Before you write a word, the questions are:

What is my purpose for this scene?

What emotional response do I want to evoke?

To accomplish that reaction, how much does the reader need to know?

How do I set it up?

Pretentiousness, clutter, and cleverness can wreck a good story. I recommend that every writer read William Zinsser's *On Writing Well,* wise words on simplicity and clarity. In the first draft I *strongly* recommended, but then I remembered Zinsser's saying qualifiers dilute persuasiveness. If I'm sincere, my recommendation doesn't have to be measured. He will also tell you not to write, "She clenched her teeth *tightly,*" because how else could she clench her teeth, for pity's sake?

While working on this manuscript, I had to make an airline reservation. When the phone voice said, "Wait a brief moment . . ." I not only laughed, but asked him if that was shorter than a moment. He pulled the plug. I wrote "brief moment" in my notebook before starting the reservation process all over again.

One of the questions I am most frequently asked by beginning writers is: Should I let my story flow, writing it straight through to the end, and then go back to polish it, or should I stay with a paragraph, a page, a word until I've found exactly the right language and I'm satisfied with it? I've formed opinions from personal experience and observing other writers at work, but there is no right or wrong answer, except the one that keeps you from becoming a nail biter.

In workshops, people writing their first novel are more apt to say they feel an urge to get the whole story down, going back to "fix it" after they've proved to themselves they have a complete story to tell. As you go along, you will find your own comfort level. Virginia says she looks at her first draft, done on a legal pad, as a sketch an artist would make before he began to enlarge the subjects, paint the colors. She usually has many sketches before she puts the scene into her word processor. The hardest part is taking out what she likes when it doesn't accomplish anything, especially when it's funny.

After I've found my character, learned enough about her story to know where I will stop it, I tend to break the story into small bites, chewing slowly on one scene at a time. Usually the flavor improves over time, but sometimes I find quite early there is nothing more I can do and move on. It's like a stick of gum after the taste is gone.

Recently, I had a minor character who was to play an important role in the plot, but I had not fleshed her out. I knew her name was Dori. She had heavy red hair, cut in irregular shaggy hunks like a Raggedy Ann doll's. She often embarrassed herself by snorting when she laughed, and she laughed a lot because she found the world a ridiculous place, but that was all I knew . . . until one morning, glancing at the paper before I started to work, I saw an article about a circus coming to town. The reporter had interviewed a clown. An epiphany! Of course, my character made her living as a clown. Perfect!

Writing in sequence, as I suggest you do, I hadn't reached the point when Dori was to be introduced, but for the next few weeks she was always on my mind. Suddenly I found clowns everywhere—in magazines, newspapers, on the telly. Language stuck to me like the sticky strips my mother used to hang to catch flies. Words to describe her goofy dancing: "Her flying limbs appeared to have a life independent of the torso to which they were attached. Then the umbrella she was carrying snapped open and started tugging everything— limbs and torso—skyward." I had a feeling for why clowns' predictable pranks please, why an angry woman like Dori would need to wear a big red nose before she could act goofy. I had the words. When I finally wrote the scene, it was a breeze, and I know a lot more about clowns.

SHADES OF MEANING

Collect words as if they were rare coins. You will know you are thinking like a writer when you itch to grab your notebook as a friend calls her poodle "snookums," or while your boss is having a tantrum, in your mind you are coolly trying to choose among "bratty," "truculent," "bellicose," "pugnacious," "hostile," "contentious," "aggressive," "combative," "belligerent," to describe his behavior.

Synonyms have roughly the same meaning, but there are subtle shades of meaning. The language you choose to put in your character's mouth will not only add nuance but reveal sex, education, attitude (tone), age, experience, position. In the situation involving the boss pitching a fit, a student intern who drew on her experience might see the angry boss being as bratty as her thirteen-year-old brother, while the Harvard M.B.A. on his staff sees him as pugnacious, but the timid guy worrying about being fired views him as hostile.

If you are creating a scene involving an altercation between a cop and a suspect in which your intent is to imply police brutality, you can say the officer pummeled, bruised, clubbed, battered, trounced, pounded, thrashed, flogged, roughed up, but if you do not intend to create an emotional effect that will place a judgment on the policeman's conduct, you could say he hit him, which doesn't carry as much of a wallop.

What if you were writing a scene involving someone who was feeling lonely? Start with the setting. Would it be more effective to have her alone in a deserted place, where maybe the telephone was out of order? Or would it be more convincing if she were in a crowd at a party, an outdoor concert where everyone except her appeared to have someone to talk to? Is it night, early morning? How strong do you want this emotion to be? Does she simply have the blues and the moment will pass, or is she depressed, maybe suicidal? Which of the following words would express the appropriate degree of her emotional state?

ennui	rejected	friendless
bleak	gloomy	forsaken
forlorn	melancholy	despair
morose	despondent	pathetic
dejected	woeful	tragic
wretched	disconsolate	pitiful

The natural phenomenon, survival of the fittest, might add chaos to society, but it explains why sports and war language permeate our thoughts and speech. When Churchill attributed the winning of World War II to what soldiers had learned on the playing fields, he was onto more than a good oxymoron. Test his theory the next time you play tennis or golf with a friend, don't forget your notebook, and remember, you are a method actor. Think from your character's point of view. Look for your character's motivation.

If his opponent is winning, does he feel competitive, antagonistic, combative, aggressive, paranoid, jealous, envious, scared? Does he think it's just a game? Does he want to break the other guy's arm? Does he notice for the first time that his opponent's eyes are as beady as a weasel's? Does he remember old, unsettled scores, such as when his buddy didn't pay his part of the bar bill or went after a woman he liked?

To determine how to shade your character's feelings, find his motivation. His father raised him to be fiercely competitive, and he appreciates it? A coach made an impression he can't shake, and he resents it? It's a dog-eat-dog world, and winning is what is most important? Being competitive has always paid off for him personally and professionally? Other aspects of his life make him secure enough not to care about a game? Knowing his degree of competitiveness and what motivates him will help you see how he will act in other situations in the story.

EXERCISES

- Someone in your character's family or office is particular and exacting. Describe her, using one of the following to shade the degree of her characteristic and to set the tone you intend:

  finicky   dainty   precise
  persnickety   fussy   picky
  fastidious   meticulous

- All characters do not cry in the same manner. Choose the

word that best describes your character's behavior but also reveals his character:

weep	wail	shriek
sob	whimper	blubber
whine	moan	sniffle

☞ Your character would call a law enforcement officer:

flatfoot	lawman	policeman
cop	patrolman	the man
pig	the fuzz	officer

☞ Your character is in a crowded place. Looking around at all the people, she sees a:

mob	swarm	congregation
pack	multitude	crowd
gang	assembly	throng
horde	crew	rabble

☞ In a range from indifferent to obsessive, find one word that would reflect the magnitude of your character's feeling toward her child or animal.

☞ A member of your character's family is not dependable. He would describe her as:

reckless	careless	imprudent
wild	daring	rash
impulsive	foolhardy	thoughtless
brash	frantic	

☞ Your character works for someone she doesn't understand. She finds him:

enigmatic	puzzling	mysterious
paradoxical	cryptic	clandestine
baffling	worrisome	

☞ Your character has a temper. From white heat to warm, find the proper degree.

☞ One of your minor characters is timid. The best way to describe his timidity would be to say he was:

apprehensive	fainthearted	mousy
pusillanimous	cowardly	shy
nonassertive	bashful	retiring

☞ In the night, your character is awakened by an abrasive sound. Which of the following qualifiers would create more tension in your story:

squawking	*penetrating*	*shrieking*
piercing	*shrill*	*blasting*
screeching	*thunderous*	*erupting*
loud	*blaring*	*booming*

☞ Your character has another profession, but he dabbles in the arts. He collects miniatures, attends exhibitions, and occasionally tries his hand at watercolors. You would describe him as:

amateur	*neophyte*	*tyro*
dilettante	*novice*	*hack*

☞ In a new dress, your character looks:

beautiful	*lovely*	*stunning*
exquisite	*gorgeous*	*cute*
captivating	*sweet*	*divine*
awesome	*pretty*	*elegant*

Maria tried the new-dress exercise on Kitty. It developed into a scene where Kitty, getting ready for a date with a man in the mob, tries on all the party dresses in her closet and talks about what dress she would wear with what man in her life. She finally chooses one that looks dangerous.

DESCRIPTIVE DETAILS

When your character is welcoming a reader to her world, you are obliged not only to give a sense of place and time, but to choose language that shows how your character views her world and herself. If she lives in a small Midwestern town, does she see it as a rinky-dink place filled with nosy people who talk about you when your back is turned, or as a peaceful hamlet where you can always find someone to pull you out of the ditch? Does she view her figure as her fortune or does she try a different crash diet every Monday morning? When he looks at his carefully tended lawn, does he see the golf course he would be on if he didn't fear his wife's wrath, a place that proves he is better at everything than the guy next door, an example of how hard work brings satisfaction, evidence of how far he has come from where he started?

You will want to create images to give your reader a visual journey, but choose graphic details with a purpose. Slimy green not only is a strong color, but also implies tackiness. Dressing your character in a suit or dress that someone sees as slimy green sends a message about either the viewer or the clothing.

Julie put a cat in her kitchen scene, not just any cat, but one her character picked up to pet, even though it shed on her business suit. The character fed her *kidney*-flavored food from a small, fancy can. The animal is not important, probably won't appear again in the story, but the details showing the character's reaction softens the sardonic tone of her wit and anticipates the care she will take in preparing the meal for her husband. The cat's gratitude, the husband's indifference, are subtle touches.

Test this. I tell you a young man drives a pickup truck. How does your reaction change if I say he drives a rusty pickup truck? Or a silver pickup with air horns? A pickup with a rifle rack?

Would you want your daughter to marry the man who drives a BMW whose interior appears to have been vacuumed every morning, a 1957 perfectly restored T-bird, a tired old Chevy with one headlight missing, a late-model, four-door black sedan? Good stories often provide the not-what-you-expect element—like the BMW owner would be a serial killer of prostitutes who sweeps the car each morning to clear away evidence, or the guy who drives with one headlight is too busy becoming the next Jasper Johns to go to the garage—but without more information, the descriptive details have created an impression and raised an expectation.

Think of yourself as a painter. Your purpose is to present a picture. What do artists use to elicit an emotional response? Start with focus. Where do you want the reader to look? What do you want him to see? What do you want her to feel? What tone are you striving to accomplish? Shade the language to draw attention to the heart of your scene or character. Structure will frame the incident.

The right detail—a gaunt face, a sick bird, an unironed shirt, bowed legs, a sinkful of dirty dishes, an uncluttered desk, a weak handshake—can add just the right effect. Too many details can spoil the mix like a heavy hand with the salt. In most cases, one adjective, one clause, one phrase will do. Leave "the softly twinkling twilight casting a pale gold glow on her pearly skin as smooth as silk" for the romance writers.

- ↪ Describe your character's car, giving details that would enable someone to spot it in an airport parking lot.
- ↪ Describe your character's car in a way that tells more about your character than her car.
- ↪ Describe the engagement ring your character gives or receives that tells more than the design, size, and type of stone.
- ↪ Your character is wearing an ugly dress. Give details to let your reader see why it is ugly.
- ↪ Your character meets an ugly man. Describe what makes him unattractive.
- ↪ Your character knows someone who has an ugly habit. Show it.
- ↪ Your character sees a bleak scene on the street. Who is involved? When? Where? How strongly is he affected?
- ↪ Your character opens a present she doesn't like. Who gave it to her? What is it? How big? What color? Shape? Style? Show her reaction.
- ↪ Your character receives the gift she has always wanted. What is it? Why did she want it? Who sent it?
- ↪ Your character watches a parade. Recount what he sees and/or feels.
- ↪ Your character is in a messy room. Picture it.
- ↪ Your character leans into the mirror. She smiles/frowns at _____.
- ↪ Your character wakes up to the smell of coffee perking. Describe her reaction.
- ↪ What color is:

Sunday	*loneliness*
your character's dream car	*joy*
contentment	*spring*
Vermont	*Italy*
friendship	*heaven*
pregnancy	*rejection*
a lollipop	*childhood*

☞ Add details to turn the following into clear images:

a desk	a hat
a flower	a bowl
a bedspread	a kitchen
a slap	a rainstorm
a barn	a stranger
a Saturday	a summer
a fish	a cake
a restaurant	a cobbler
a meal	a drink
a stripper	a snob
an order	a dancer
a soldier	a baby
a game	a beggar
a disappointment	a holiday
a wallet	a comfort
a spinnaker	a fear
a cup of tea	a mosquito
a gun	a stuffed animal
a belly	a sound

John worked the exercise describing a slap into an incident to show a mother's ferocious need to control her adult son. Grasping his chin with her left hand, she slapped him with her more powerful right.

DIALOGUE

Some writers are born with ears that remember. Others have to train them. Men and women, rich and poor, old and young, disillusioned and hopeful, powerful and weak, intelligent and slow-witted, braggarts and meek people, do not speak the same language. Hear like a writer. Make a mental recording of how people's language reflects their ideas and attitudes. As they speak, notice gestures, facial expressions, pauses, cadence.

Try to remember your father's voice when he was giving you advice or lecturing. Dialogue is more than words. What contributed to the stern tone? Did he ramble, showing his discomfort, or come precisely to the point, as if he had been rehearsing? Was it words or body language that got your attention? What happened to his shoulders? What did he do with his hands? Did he look you in the eye or focus on the ceiling? Did you have the impression he was feeling powerful or miserable? Did he come to your room? Summon you to his study? Or were war councils always held around the kitchen table? You want to let your reader see your characters talking.

How do you make a character sound old? You can use "in my day" or "when I was young" only occasionally. An older person is more apt to long for "a nice cup of tea," while a health-conscious, young person will have a theory about what herbal or peppermint tea leaves will do for his digestion, bones, or biceps. The elderly are often frustrated or impatient because they can't remember a name, a fact, a telephone number. As they watch others taking over responsibility for running the family, the business, the government, the world, old people's language reflects their loss of power and control. They tend to reminisce. As you put words into their mouths, think about their attitude toward their next stage—death.

When you begin to write dialogue, refer to the exercises you did to learn more about your character's interests, fears, hopes, etc. If he raises flowers, floral images like "a face as innocent as a pansy" will appear in his speech, while if she has season tickets to the Mets, she might say, "My only hope is a slide or a steal."

Two women the same age, even sisters, have to sound different. You should not have to add the tag "Jane said," "Polly said," each time one of them speaks. After you have established who is talking to whom, a reader should recognize Jane's sarcasm or Polly's timidity from what she says and her mannerisms. The women miss their plane. Jane's response: "There goes the first on-time departure in the history of this airline." She shakes her fist at the plane's tail. "They're going to hear from me." But Polly says, "Oh, please don't make a fuss. They'll remember and be horrid to us the next time we fly."

If you have found the right words, the language should set the tone, so you do not have to explain the intended attitude or manner. Polly's words reflect her unassertive nature. No reason to add "she said timidly." If a character says, "I'm in love with someone else," there is a need to know the tone, but there are more effective ways to accomplish this than by adding "he said indifferently." Have him glance at his watch, look at the wall when she cries, move away from her. SHOW, DON'T TELL.

Show what your character is thinking as well as what he is saying. In the workshop, Marc's character Larry—a hotshot lawyer—has just been fired. He needs support. Late at night, driving with his friend Jack, he hits a beaver. Nipping into Larry's thoughts as he speaks, we learn he would not have stopped, but he senses that Jack thinks he should. It is his need for his friend's approval, not his concern for a squashed animal, that moves him to wrap the beaver in his expensive leather jacket and put it in the trunk of the car.

If you've discovered a character you're crazy about, showing the complexity of his personality can be a problem. The tendency is to become overly protective, hesitant about showing his weaknesses and flaws. In the scene above, Marc didn't turn Larry into an unsympathetic character but made him human, a guy who has motives, needs, and urges as ambiguous and conflicting as the reader's. Finding those universal feelings—jealousy, fear, rage, need, lack of confidence—and presenting them in a fresh way is what makes a good story. Editors, agents, and readers are not in the market for a story about the perfect person who never has a run in her stocking.

Even the best dialogue can't carry a scene on its own. Jealousy is a powerful force in a story, but the language is difficult. Writing about Andy and Sue, a lesbian couple, Heather put them at a party with guests both gay and straight, playing the game Truth or Dare. When Sue's dare is to French-kiss Ron, the reader experiences it from Andy's viewpoint. The dialogue and the action are passionate, charged, but would not have had as strong an impact if we were not also experiencing Andy's painful and angry thoughts and feelings.

Avoid corny language unless you want your character to be obviously corny. A sappy teenage girl extravagantly in love could say, "When he touches me I get big fat goose pimples and see bright twinkling stars," but avoid shivers, visions, and double adjectives for a mature character you are trying to portray sympathetically.

Generally, it is not wise to produce speech that looks funny on the page—many dots, dashes, and weird spellings. If you're in Topeka creating a minor character from Georgia, you'll have better luck simply saying she has a Southern drawl or accent, perhaps revealing your character's response to the vernacular rather than trying to spell "you all" the way they say it in Georgia. I suggest you follow the same pattern for speech afflictions and infirmities. This is one of the few times when telling works better than showing.

In the fourth or fifth grade we learned to place only what someone speaks aloud in quotation marks. Thoughts are not quoted, but are punctuated as narrative. The same rule applies to interior monologues or internal debates between your character and her conscience. However, you will resort to ellipses if you are using *stream of consciousness,* a technique used by Dostoyevsky and Henry James, but perfected by James Joyce. The idea is to capture the raw flow of consciousness with its perceptions, thoughts, judgments, feelings, associations, and memories presented just as they occur, without being tidied into grammatical sentences or given logical and narrative order. The method attempts the exact reproduction of consciousness, but since sense perceptions, feelings, and even aspects of thought are nonverbal, the writer must convert these elements into words, and much of this conversion is a matter of convention rather than of point-by-point reproduction. Italicizing an interior monologue alerts the reader. To see how others have done it, look at work by William Faulkner or Virginia Woolf, or read Molly Bloom's famous forty-two-page interior monologue in Joyce's *Ulysses*.

Writers talk about dreaming from the viewpoint of their characters, arguments they have, scoldings they give or receive. If you know your character that well, the following exercises will be a snap. If you are not certain what your character would say or how she would feel in these situations, don't despair. Dig a little deeper into her backstory. Think about what she wants. Most important, think about what hurdles stand in her way.

E X E R C I S E S

- ☞ When asked to define home, your character says _____ _____.

- ☞ His boss smiles as he says, "Sorry, old boy, you're not invited." Your character says _____ but he thinks _____.

- A child tells your character he hates her. She responds _____. Describe her facial expression and her body language as she speaks.

- "I will never forget _____," your character says.

- "Before I die, I want to _____," your character says.

- "I will tell you about _____, but I would perish if _____ were to find out," your character says.

- "If I had the gumption, I would _____," your character says when _____.

- If she had not had a bad day, your character might not have said "_____."

- Asked to speak at his memorial, your character said, "_____."

- The nastiest thing your character ever said was _____.

- When the doctor said, "Your father died," your character said, "_____," as he thought _____.

- Your character steps on a snake. She says, "_____."

- When your character's lover says she feels like making love, your character says, "_____."

- Write a conversation between him and a colleague when your character has something to hide.

- Write a conversation between your character and her husband or lover when she has something to hide.

- Write a conversation between your character and a garage mechanic when the car is not ready.

- Write a conversation between your character and a cabdriver on a day when she is feeling as if luck has taken a holiday.

- Write a telephone conversation between your character and his mother.

- Write a conversation between your character and her best friend discussing a family matter. Use discriminating speech patterns, establish an attitude, to set them apart.

- Write a conversation between a young couple. One of them wants to break up. The other argues to continue the relationship. Use language that indicates sex and age.

- "The stock market fell a hundred fucking points today," his broker says. Your character says, "_____."

- Your character meets someone who has a speech defect. She stutters, stammers, or is pathologically shy. Create a dialogue between them that allows the reader to get the picture without your actually reproducing the afflicted person's speech pattern.

- The judge asks for the defense. Write it from your character's or his lawyer's point of view.

- Your character is in a life-threatening situation. Write an interior monologue.

- Your character, a mild-mannered person who is having difficulty meeting the mortgage payments, goes to dinner with someone who keeps saying things like, "The next time you get to Paris, you must try _____."

Writing a flashback to a childhood conversation between a minor character and his mother as she helped him with his homework, John had her say, "Gotya." Smacking his head, John said, "Of course! That's what she's been doing to him all his life. That's why he doesn't have enough confidence to stand up to his wife."

VERBS, ADVERBS, AND UNNECESSARY ADJECTIVES

Most passive verbs belong in the same rubbish bin with cliches. Unless you can find no logical way around it, avoid the passive voice. It lacks spunk, gumption, vigor, drive, and usually courage. If you write, "He had been ruined by the office gossip," the reader is not certain who has done what to whom. "The office gossip ruined him" has more punch.

You can use the passive voice to develop a wishy-washy character or one who does not want to take responsibility for anything, even his own words. Oliver North learned the trick from Nixon, who became a master of the passive voice during Watergate. "The tapes were erased by mistake." Who is *mis-*

take? "The order came from above." Is *above* God, Reagan, Casey, Bush, Poindexter? Your character who says, "Rumors about him have been heard," ducks being held accountable. The one who says, "I've heard rumors about him," looks you in the eye when he speaks.

Verbs show action. "Mary slapped his sneering face." The reader knows exactly what has happened, sees the picture immediately. "His sneering face was slapped by Mary" is longer, less clear, and the action has lost its vigor.

Writers have to be as sensitive to language as firemen to smoke, especially when choosing verbs, your power tools. Don't settle for a walk with a home-run hitter in the dugout.

Verbs can sharpen an image. "She squashed the cockroach with her heel" has more intensity than "She stepped on the cockroach with her heel." "Squashed" also sounds like what it means. So do "pamper," "swish," "screech," "moan," "slaughter," "whine," "sass," "hiss," "spit." When they don't want to frighten you, commercial pilots might say, "The airplane lost altitude," but if your character is in that aluminum capsule free-falling, you can find a word with more oomph. Why pick a boring wimp of a verb? Our language abounds with colorful and musical action words.

Try for precision. Don't send someone to the happy hunting ground when you can kill him. Losing her job might feel like death, but "she was terminated" does not give as accurate a picture as "she was fired." "He fired her" is even better, not only because this tells who did it, but verbs without auxiliaries ("was") are more sharply focused. "Was fired" indicates indefinite time, whereas "fired" suggests a given moment.

Euphemistic expressions—like a dead man being given "his just reward," or the woman who is lying when she says she has to "powder her nose"—can be effective when you're poking fun at a prude, prig, fuddy-duddy, or nitpicker, but unless you want to sound like a puritan, use verbs that say what they mean.

Nouns as well as verbs can be diluted or made perfectly silly by the euphemistic, a phony approach to gentility. In a *New Yorker* essay, novelist Bobbie Ann Mason said in the South cocks were called boy chickens and bulls were male cows, but she was being ironic. If you just can't call a penis a penis and your typewriter won't write any form of the verb "to die," maybe you'd better talk to someone besides the IBM repairman.

Good storytellers strive for vivacious characters and vivid

pictures. Focus, just as if you were snapping a picture. "She saw that the boy had pulled his knife, cutting the girl's thumb" becomes more vibrant if we directly see the action rather than filter it through another character's view. "The boy pulled his blade and slashed the girl's thumb."

Varying the length and structure of your sentences is important, but avoid overusing or illogically beginning sentences with participles and infinitive phrases, such as, "Running down the road in fear, she jumped into the empty car and drove away, not caring whose it might be." Quite a trick. Better to say, "She ran down the road. When she saw the empty car, she was so scared she jumped in and drove away, not caring whose it might be."

Few absolute rules exist for writing fiction, so I won't say all adverbs are unnecessary. I accumulate emphatic ones like "egregiously" and "unabashedly." But beware. When your character slams the door, there is no need to add "loudly." Doors just won't slam softly. If you have shown an action and still feel that you must qualify how it was done, the scene might need to be reworked. Beginning writers are especially prone to adding a redundant modifier to how a character says something. "My beautiful wife has cancer," he said sadly. "My God, he's going to kill me," she said nervously. "Almost frantic," "sort of happy," "totally astounded," weaken the impact.

When words come out of your character's mouth, they say them. They don't smile, laugh, grunt, or cry them out. Delete " 'I'm delighted to meet you,' she smiled." She might say it with a smile on her face or tears in her eyes, her tone might sound like a grunt, but what she does is say the words. Including the obvious, the illogical, or the redundant sends a message of sloppy or careless writing to editors, agents, readers—the people you care about most.

Adjectives have a better reputation than adverbs, but some silly ones like "a little bit pregnant" have been known to do more harm than good. In a *New York Times Magazine* column, Jack Hersch complained about a doctor's diagnosing his son as suffering from "mild" cerebral palsy, which he said was like hearing your wife was in a "mild" plane crash or a "mild" tornado had struck.

"Nice" has the strong punch of a snowflake. If you can't find anything to say except "nice dinner," "nice date," "nice boy," "nice time," turn off your computer, take a walk, and have a "nice day."

"Slightly" has been known to have slightly any meaning at all. What exactly does "slightly hungry," "slightly sleepy," "slightly cold," "slightly scared," mean?

    Find vivid verbs to intensify the following situations:

a *bike accident*	a *roller-coaster ride*
a *falling star*	a *voice calling 911*
a *stalker*	a *fiery sermon*
a *rainstorm*	a *faulty muffler*
baby's first step	*fear of the dark*
a *slick road*	a *coward's challenge*
a *man on a ledge*	*two out in the bottom*
the voice of a duck	*of the ninth*

    Revise the following:

The final blow was delivered by her mother.

She noticed that she didn't feel the same about Mark anymore. His conversation was boring. His ties irritated her.

He felt sort of blue. A wee bit tired and completely bored.

"My baby was born with the cord wrapped around her neck," she said sadly.

"What do you want?" she questioned.

Jane's boss stepped down.

They were scheduled to tie the knot at midnight.

"I'm crazy about you," Madge whispered softly into his ear.

"I was almost scared."

"I'm absolutely flabbergasted."

"He is a good boy, and he has a nice father."

Turning to her boss, who was saying dreadful things, she wished she were big enough to punch him in the nose. Breaking a pencil she held tightly in her hand and thinking bad thoughts, she went to lunch while he was still talking.

FIGURATIVE LANGUAGE

All language is symbolic, but literal language follows a standard form and attempts to tell the truth without exaggeration or flourish. The sky is blue. Mary died. John walks fast. Figurative language departs from standard construction, order, and significance of words to achieve special meaning or effect. John walks as if his shoes have jet engines. Not only poets, but all of us use figures of speech in conversation and writing. We make comparisons, exaggerate for emphasis, use words symbolically and humorously. Unfortunately, most of us liberally sprinkle our conversation with clichés, figures of speech used so often they have become trite and tedious, like: "green as grass," "nipped in the bud," "hotter than hell," "feet of clay," "everything is coming up roses," "Mary passed on to a better world." In your story, avoid clichés "like the plague" (including this one). They are poison. Poet Alexander Pope says:

> Where'er you find "the cooling western breeze,"
> In the next line it "whispers through the trees";
> If crystal streams "with pleasing murmurs creep,"
> The reader threatened (not in vain) with "sleep."

To refresh your memory, the following defines figures of speech you might be able to use in your novel.

A **simile**, a comparison between two essentially different items, is indicated by terms such as "like" or "as." "On Sunday, time moves as slowly as my grandfather." "Uninvited, he flopped on my swimming towel like a beached whale." "She acts haunted, like a Holocaust survivor with numbers tattooed on her arm." "His bald head looked as if it had been polished with floor wax." "He can be as comforting as a wet sleeping bag."

In a **metaphor**, a word which in ordinary usage signifies one kind of thing, quality, or action is applied to another, without an expressed indication of a relation between them. "The vice president of human resources was the company's killer bee." "The engagement ring with an exceptionally large stone closed the sale." "Luck is the residue of design." "He was tanned to the color of her lizard handbag." "The despairing soul is a rebel." "Welfare cowboys graze their cattle on government land." "Stunt pilots strap in so tightly, they are wearing the plane."

An **image** or **imagery** has come to mean more than a mental picture. The most common meaning is a signifier of figurative language, especially metaphors and similes, or image clusters (recurrent groups of figures) that create image motifs or thematic imagery, like the frequent use of figures of sickness, disease, and corruption in *Hamlet.*

In the following, notice how Saul Bellow uses a combination of cold nature images and hot human pictures in his poetic prayer:

> Snowbound, I watched the blizzard impounding parked cars at midnight. The veering of the snowflakes under the street lights made me think how nice it would be if we were totally covered by white drifts. Give us a week's moratorium, dear Lord, from the idiocies that burn on every side and let the pure snows cool these overheated minds and dilute the toxins which have infected our judgments. Grant us a breather, merciful God.

Personification is a figure closely related to metaphor. An inanimate object or an abstract concept is described as having human qualities, powers, or feelings. "My typewriter sulked." "The summer of '83 had it in for me." "Even my frisky puppy was singing the blues." In certain parts of the country where bodies of water, mountains, forests, play such an important part in how people make a living or in the quality of their lives, they take on powerful human qualities, as this headline indicates: "The Mighty Mississippi Won Another Round." In other parts of the country, Wall Street and the Dow Jones industrial average assume life-giving and life-threatening significance. Newspapers report, "The Dow stumbles"; "Wall Street holds its breath."

A **pun** is a play on words that are identical or similar in sound but have sharply diverse meanings. "At night, when you are lonely, what a difference a knight can make." In Maine, where the number of treasured loons is threatened, a watchdog committee calls itself "The Loon Rangers." Perhaps you would have to live in Chicago to see humorous possibilities with Marshall Field and Field Marshal So-and-So.

Or a pun can be the use of a single word or phrase with two incongruous meanings, both relevant. "Check my check for the amount I paid."

Children and advertisers love puns. Recently, Madison Avenue punsters invented Lester Sweet to promote a less sweet soda pop. A company that sells soap is having fun with people who take "tossing the salad" literally. I realize puns are hard to resist, but if the urge strikes you when you're writing, unless it is a sure winner, use it to entertain the kids.

A **paradox** is a statement that seems absurd or self-contradictory but which turns out to have a tenable and coherent meaning, as in the conclusion to Donne's sonnet on death:

> *One short sleep past, we wake eternally,*
> *And death shall be no more; Death, thou shalt die.*

An **oxymoron** is a paradoxical statement that juxtaposes words or terms that in ordinary usage are contraries: "John had a repellent fascination for her," or "Missing you is pleasing pain." My editor with an uppity pet called "cat's gratitude." A cynic I know offered "postal service" and "military intelligence." My favorite is "happy ending."

Alliteration is the repetition of any consonant or vowel sound, especially at the beginning of words or in stressed syllables. "Silly sister," "gangly guy," "cuddly cat," "enigmatic egotist."

Allusion is a brief reference to a person, place, or event assumed to be sufficiently well known to be recognized by the reader. Characters in literature ranging from Helen of Troy and Ophelia to Scarlett O'Hara and Blanche DuBois need no introduction.

Allegory converts a doctrine or thesis into a narrative in which the agents, and sometimes the setting, represent general concepts, moral qualities, or other abstractions. In Bunyan's *the Pilgrim's Progress*, Christian, fleeing from the City of Destruction, goes through places such as Slough of Despond and Vanity Fair, where he meets characters like Worldly-Wiseman. Caution is advised. That was then; this is now. However, in a 1993 publication, Jack Butler did have the Holy Ghost narrate his novel, *Living in Little Rock with Miss Little Rock;* and in his highly praised novel, *Cape of Storms,* Afrikaner André Brink deals with apartheid in an extremely polemical allegory of the relationship between dissimilar races and cultures. But allegory, if used heavy-handedly, can become didactic and give the impression the writer is preaching.

Figurative language that comes spontaneously, growing naturally out of your plot or character, will add interest but can wreck good writing if overused, or if it appears to be an affectation. For example, if you are creating a stiff, regimented, by-the-book-type character, military images could help reveal his nature, but figurative language should not work like stop signs, causing a reader to pause, ponder, and lose the flow of the story. When a figure of speech calls attention to itself, no matter how clever you think it is, zap it.

The following warm-up exercises are intended to make you more aware of the language possibilities, not to encourage artificial means of expression.

E X E R C I S E S

- ↝ The contents of your character's purse are like a _____ _____.

- ↝ "Your mind is a _____," your character says to _____.

- ↝ Your character compares his pet with a politician.

- ↝ Your character compares the other woman with a _____.

- ↝ Create a metaphor for your character's backache.

- ↝ Personify your character's fax machine.

- ↝ Personify a storm.

- ↝ Personify the stock-market ticker tape.

- ↝ Personify your character's broom closet.

- ↝ Your character gives an allegorical name to the place where she lives or works.

- ↝ Write an interior monologue in which your character alludes to an actual person or fictional character she admires, wondering how he would solve her dilemma.

- ↝ Add to the following list of words that have a literal and a metaphorical meaning:

doormat	*frame*	*sleeper*
spearhead	*chisel*	*hairpin*

- ↝ Make a pun out of corn.

- ↝ Make a pun with soul.

- ↝ Find a pun for your son.

- ↝ Find an oxymoron to explain your character's preference for unhealthy food.

- ↝ Use alliteration to describe your character's:

car	*love affair*
running gait	*bathrobe*

WRITING STYLES THAT AFFECT TONE

Hyperbole is extravagant exaggeration, a style of writing that consciously overstates without the intention of literal persuasion. You may use it sparingly in figures of speech to heighten effect, as in "The news hit like a bullet between his eyes." You might also use the style for comic effect, like, "His wet, sloppy kisses reminded her of the dingy string mop she had recently been dragging across Mrs. Brown's sticky kitchen floor."

You could say, "The news upset him," or "She didn't enjoy his kiss," but high-flown language contains an emotional impact and suggestions not necessarily present in the object or event.

Think of your aunt Millie, who described a rain shower in terms that could encourage the cautious to build an ark; or your boss, who blows your slightest mistake into a blimp; or your teenage daughter's description of the guy who is an answer to her dreams; or the woman in the doctor's office who described her colostomy in terms that could have been used in a horror movie.

The tall tale and tall talk of the American Southwest are forms of comic hyperbole. In his *Glossary of Literary Terms*, M. H. Abrams uses one I especially like: "There was the cowboy in an Eastern restaurant who ordered a steak well done. 'Do you call this well done?' he roared at the waitress. 'I've seen critters hurt worse than that get well!' "

The opposite extreme is **understatement**, a form of irony in which something is intentionally represented as less than in fact it is, such as Jonathan Swift's saying, "Last week I saw a woman flayed, and you will hardly believe how much it altered her appearance for the worse."

Understatement is often used for humorous or satiric effect, as was Twain's intent when he said, "The reports of my death are greatly exaggerated."

Writers also understate for emphasis. Let's say you have written a convincing love story. You have advanced the plot through trials the couple had to overcome, developed the characters enough for the reader to have realized the richness of the life they shared, but the woman dies. The man says, "I miss her." The sparse, clipped language spoken with no stated inflection can be effective. He implies more than he says by stating his feelings less strongly than the case will allow. The reader's imagination kicks in, bringing the past to bear on the present and predicting the future.

Camus's classic, understated style made his stranger familiar to a multitude of readers when he opened his novel: "Mother died today. Or, maybe, yesterday; I can't be sure."

Hyperbole that exaggerates and understatement that minimizes are distorted styles. Between the two lies the undistorted style, which simply tries to tell it and show it like it is. This middle style operates from the old premise that fiction holds a mirror up to reality.

Irony is a manner of speaking in which the implied attitude or evaluation is opposed to what is literally expressed. "I grieve to think you're leaving," a desperate host says to a monstrous houseguest. Ostensible praise or approval implying dispraise or disapproval is used more frequently than the reverse form.

The writer who uses irony displays an implicit high regard for her audience. The ironic style can be extremely complex. By assuming his readers get it, without even a facial expression or vocal intonation, the writer is paying them a compliment. The ability to recognize irony is one of the surest tests of intelligence and sophistication. If a political prisoner in a foreign country whose mail is censored writes to his American wife, "I have the same high regard for my captors as the citizens of Atlanta had for General Sherman," he is banking on his wife's knowledge and his captor's ignorance of American history. They, not she, will be taken in by the literal meaning.

You can use irony for humor and to expose the obtuseness of other characters who are fooled by the subtlety. Take the woman who has a blind date with a guy who appears in a gaudy floral polyester shirt, showing five gold chains on his chest. She says, "I've always been intrigued by baroque fashions for men." He smiles and thanks her.

Irony and sarcasm are kissing cousins, not synonyms. Sarcasm is a caustic and bitter expression of personal disapproval disguised as apparent praise. It is personal, jeering, and intended to hurt, like a sneering taunt. A sarcastic boss might say to an employee who has made a mistake, "Oh, you're a prince, a real prince." Irony is usually lighter in its wording, but more cutting because of its indirectness. The ironic writer has a sort of grim humor, an unemotional detachment. He shows a coolness in expression when his emotions are heated. The effectiveness of irony as a literary device is the impression it gives of great restraint. Mark Antony's insistence in his funeral oration that "Brutus is an honorable man" is a classic example.

Satire diminishes a subject by making it ridiculous and evoking toward it attitudes of amusement, contempt, or scorn. While comedy evokes laughter as an end in itself, satire derides, using laughter as a weapon against a butt. The target may be an individual, a type of person, a class, a nation, an established institution, or even the whole human race. One of the most savage examples is in Jonathan Swift's "modest proposal" for saving a starving Ireland by selling the country's babies to the English for food. Read Jane Austen for less brutal examples.

Those who write satire most often justify it as a means of correcting vice and folly by exposure. Many writers whose overall intent is not satiric will satirize a certain character or situation, but in many great literary achievements satire—diminishing a subject by ridicule—is the organizing principle of the entire story.

In your story you might create one incident to satirize the IRS's intimidation tactics when your character is harassed because he figured his income tax incorrectly, or you might write a horror-story scene about an air carrier losing his baggage or canceling an important flight. However, if your purpose is to satirize the agency or industry, the ridiculous, unfair, or cruel practices must dominate the action and events. Joseph Heller did an outstanding job of satirizing the air force in *Catch-22*. In the workshop, Fran can't write fast enough to keep up with the satirical material she finds for her G.I. Josephine in a bizarre army physical-training program for women.

In the same group, Maria's dominant theme is the corruption in big-city government. Even though her characters fall in love, have family relationships, everything happens under the cloud of corruption—crooked deals, cronyism, greed, manipulation. Fran's story makes you laugh; Maria's makes you cringe.

The degree of your satiric sting will be determined by your aim, tone, and, always, language. Perhaps you will simply want to evoke a smile at the foibles of a workaholic, an overly possessive lover, an obsessively protective mother. Your aim is for amusement, not indignation. Or your purpose could be to arouse contempt and moral indignation at the vices and depravity of mankind. In that case, your satiric narrator speaks from the persona of a serious moralist denouncing aberrations which are no less dangerous because they are ridiculous.

In a previous section we discussed how the naive narrator can elicit dramatic irony, allowing the more experienced reader to realize what the unsuspecting narrator's nature hides. The nonjudgmental point of view can also be effective in a satire.

Armed with a Ph.D. from Cambridge, John, a writer in the workshop, is working on an academic satire exposing pretentious practices and ridiculous traditions in higher education, as well as the absurdities brought on by English, Irish, and American nationalism. His Merk is an outrageous Irish character whose scandalous, atrocious, and humorous deeds and thoughts are motivated by people's foibles, silliness, and meanness, especially those in the elitist British academic environment. The story, told from the point of view of an American graduate student who suspends his distrust of Merk's machinations much longer than the reader, is most effective.

To be a good writer, you don't have to register a style of preference at the courthouse. Experiment, take risks, until you find the right word, the perfect tone, that express your ideas just the way you intended.

EXERCISES

- ∽ From your character's point of view, describe a mud slide or a muddy pigpen, using hyperbole either to heighten the effect or to create humor.

- ∽ Have your character relate his experience with a tornado in an understated way.

- ∽ Write a scene set in a blinding rainstorm punctuated with lightning and thunder. Try to find language to make it as realistic as possible.

- ∽ Your character dislikes her next-door neighbor. Using different styles, write her feelings in three disparate ways.

- ∽ A serial killer confesses to having murdered thirteen children. Describe him from the viewpoint of a sarcastic person. Describe the same person from an ironic point of view. Describe the killer as he would be recorded on the police department blotter.

- Have one of your minor characters tell your protagonist, in an exaggerated manner, how politics is practiced where he votes.

- Using understatement, write a scene in which your character describes police corruption or brutality in the community. Rewrite the scene from the viewpoint of someone whose purpose is to incite a riot.

- Your character takes a child to the carnival. The temperature is one hundred degrees. The child insists upon riding on all rides that go round and round. After eating cotton candy, he throws up. Your character finds a worm in his hot dog and a long gray hair wrapped around his ice-cream cone. Write the scene in an ironic style. Rewrite it using a straightforward technique.

- Your character is asked to make a speech supporting a candidate for the school board, the city council, national office. Write two versions—first, a sincere speech in which she gives his qualifications. Rewrite the address satirizing the opposition.

- Your character remembers a honeymoon during which everything possible went wrong. Write it laced with hyperbole. Try telling the same events in an ironic tone.

- Practice a variety of styles to describe the following:

a beautiful woman	*a flower garden*
an ugly baby	*a sunrise*
an injury	*a fighting fish*
a Christmas tree	*a greedy eater*
an outboard motor	*a bushy head of hair*
an applesauce cake	*a frisky cat*
a runner who loses	*a flirt*
the race	*an embarrassed adolescent*
a fistfight	*tight pants*
a family quarrel	*time*
a character's obsession	*the death of a child*
an egotist	*the end of the road*
a character's magic	*spilled milk*
a skinny man	*a bad day*

CHAPTER 9

Structuring Your Story

Structure, the overall design of your novel, is determined by several component parts which all contribute to its effectiveness. Where and when the story takes place are important structuring elements in the overall form which we will discuss farther on. Compare the difference between planning a look at five generations of a large family in South Africa and preparing to tell what happens during the first six months an actress from Idaho spends in Manhattan.

SETTING

Now that you recognize the sound of your character's voice, comprehend his attitude toward himself and others, have grasped his expectations and sense of entitlement, understand how much hope he has, you probably also know his mailing address, but that is only one aspect of the setting for your story.

The **historical period** you explore affects every consideration. Most beginning writers feel more comfortable writing in the present or the immediate past, but if the English Tudors fascinate you, and you are willing to do research, why not move your character back in time? In Henry VIII's England, people were motivated by greed, fear, love, jealousy as much as they are today. Designing exercises for the workshop presents a challenge, because Alice's story about Lucian, a Syrian sophist, is set in antiquity. If the exercise involves a car, she substitutes a chariot or a cart. When the others need a contrasting opinion, they choose someone from their characters' offices, therapy groups, or neighborhoods, while Alice usually uses Lucian's educated Greek slave or a Stoic philosopher.

In our more recent past, the sixties produced philosophers who changed America forever. Most of the leaders were young, flamboyant, verbal, controversial, and in conflict with established order. What better ingredients for a novel? All the stories have not been told about Prohibition and the Roaring Twenties, the Great Depression, World War II, the Vietnam war. And don't overlook the scandals. Watergate, the Iran Contra affair, the savings and loan failures. There are those who think the yuppies and their junk bonds were as outrageous as the hippies and their grass. Don't shy away from significant events like the assassinations of President Kennedy and Martin Luther King simply because they've been done before. There's always room for a new, unique, personal perspective. Although there have been many fine novels that did not explore the political and social issues of their time, you are writing in a time rich with possibilities.

The workshop meets in Manhattan, so most of the stories are set in the tri-state area, but there are Wayne's characters who live in the tobacco country of North Carolina. They say, "How you?", eat corn pone, and "take a whiz" when they have to pee. He is writing a **regional novel**, which emphasizes the setting, language, and mores of a particular locality. He exploits the *local color*—landscape, dialect, customs—for its inherent interest and oddity. You can do the same if the area you know is set apart by its differences.

Train your ears to remember and your eyes to take photographs. I grew up on a farm of green-and-gold fields where we raised animals that worked their way into our figures of speech. I still wouldn't buy a pig in a poke, and someone chomping on gum still looks to me like a cow chewing her cud.

Now, in the summer I go to Maine. Paint it blue. Even the mountains have absorbed the color of the sea. Down East politicians' popularity "ebbs and flows," and the worst thing you can say about someone is, "He's the kind who'd pull someone else's traps."

The **physical environment** can play an important role in your story. For instance, if you're writing about a Maine lob-

sterman's battle with the old devil sea, describing the sea-
scape and the weather will be a top priority. If your story is
set in Vermont or Colorado, you'd better know snow—how it
looks, how powder feels, how the air smells before a storm
hits, what kind of sound a spinning tire makes when it's
packed in ice. No one from Chicago calls Chicago "Second
City." Keep up your guard if you do. Some factory workers
spend hours looking at a one-inch-square vista, while the
views of commercial airline pilots or astronauts go on forever.
To create the environment, you become a method actor and
experience the ambiance. If I tried writing a novel set in a
submarine, the next one would no doubt be told from a mental institution. I'm claustrophobic. When you choose your setting, pick a place you will be willing to unpack your suitcase
in for a long stay.

Writers have cleverly used the setting as a means of bringing a group of people together who have nothing in common
other than being in a certain place at a particular time. The
characters in *Ship of Fools* and *Airplane* must interact. They
can't escape the setting. In *The Firm,* the lawyers have lives
outside, but the law office is more than a structuring device
for bringing them together; it is a villainous presence, a personality, a culture as strong as the worst scoundrel the author uses as a moral test for his characters.

You can use a setting like a church, a company, a train, a
school, a profession, a community, or a social group simply
as a means of bringing your characters together, or you can
personify the place, like, "Only a moment ago, the church
had towered above, but now it hovered over him listening
with dismay and disapproval to his knavish thoughts." In the
Victorian age, when the world moved at a slower pace and
offered fewer distractions to a reader's time, novelists devoted
pages and pages to describing the setting. Not only do Emily
Brontë's moors have a temperament as strong as the characters, but the locale has a potent influence on the characters'
actions and thoughts.

Sometimes the **spiritual background** where the action
takes place can be essential. A character's story can be
shaped by the religious, mental, moral, social, and emotional
conditions of her environment. Think of Ken Kesey's novel
One Flew Over the Cuckoo's Nest, set in a mental hospital;
Sartre's play *No Exit,* taking place in an eternal purgatory;
Thomas Mann's *Magic Mountain,* set in a rest home for pa-

tients with tuberculosis; or the exotic settings of Poe's short stories like "Murder in the Rue Morgue."

A SENSE OF PLACE

Next to the sign reminding you to Show, Don't Tell, it would be advisable to tack another placard: A Sense of Place. When you move your character from the boardroom to the corner bar at 10:30 A.M., in your mind you see him shoving his proposal that didn't sell into his tacky briefcase white with wear on the edges, walking stealthily down the hall past the corporate officers' closed doors. You know he breathes easier when the elevator is empty and he doesn't meet one familiar face until he ducks into Pete's, where Pete doesn't even glance at the clock as he stirs, without bruising, a double vodka martini with a twist. You know where your character is, what time it is, and what a scary place his imagination has become, but the reader doesn't. If the chairman's last line is "We've been patient, Harry, but your idea is too damned little too damned late," and Harry's next line is "Peter, make it a double," your reader will wonder when they starting serving liquor at board meetings.

Before you describe a setting, determine what you want from the scene other than clarity. Where's the emotional center of the situation? In the example above, is your purpose to evoke sympathy or disrespect for Harry? Are the board meeting and the chairman only ploys or props to give you reason to delve into Harry's problems? Or is your point to make the company and the men who run it indifferent, cold, or even villainous? If Harry's thoughts are the core of the scene, put him in a boardroom and forget the decor. Details describing the furniture, the color of the walls, the size of the room, the opulence or lack of it, would only distract the reader's attention. Make the chairs hard and uncomfortable, place Harry in a position where he can't hear what is going on, have the air conditioner blow frigid air on his neck only if it reinforces the painful or unfair situation you want the reader to feel.

Look for a fresh way to describe familiar settings or decor. Most readers have flown over or sailed past the Statue of Liberty—at least in their imaginations. With a little luck, they will have marveled at a full moon casting white light on a body of water. Look for language to bring a brighter view to a prosaic experience.

In some novels, after you have established where the character is, the setting has little or no significance. Any big city, small village, deserted beach, isolated farm, cruise ship, university, windowless room, will do. A general rule is, Don't waste your words giving elaborate or detailed descriptions of bedrooms, streets, offices, unless you need the details to move your plot, reveal your character, or create a necessary atmosphere or ambiance. Forget the color of the drapes unless the light shining through the red silk makes your character look ruddy, and he sits there so his mother won't notice his pale skin and realize he has AIDS. However, no matter if the story is set in Portland or Paducah, for the reader to follow the action in a murder mystery, the writer has to locate precisely where windows, doors, staircases, porn shops, etc., exist.

In the age of E-mail and airplanes, Aristotle's requirement for unity of place—the action be limited to one location—is no longer heeded. The reader will go spanning the world with you, as long as she knows where she is and why you have transported her from Tangier to Tucson. In your day job, if you travel often and think like a writer, you will fill your notebook with descriptions of interesting, exotic, beautiful, or horrifying settings. If you're lucky, one of those places will be exactly what you needed for an episode in your story. At this point you know to avoid the temptation to stick in an unnecessary scene simply because you found exquisite language to depict a sunset in the Sahara.

Raymond Carver's collection of short stories, *Where I'm Calling From*, contains stories with different geographic settings, but Carver is always calling from a place where his mind is filled with regrets. What is going on in his character's mind is more interesting than what is going on around him. Kafka's settings are inside his character's head. Dickens used the contrast of scenes in squalor and in grandeur to make a social statement. Hardy gave the heath a character and personality as strong and as interesting as his characters. Melville did the same for the sea. F. Scott Fitzgerald's settings set a pace as well as a tone. His language kept pace with rich, languid ladies lolling lazily on verandas or dancing holes in their soles to a jazzy beat. Pop-culture writers like Jackie

Collins rely on readers' fantasies about elegant homes, hotels, restaurants, designer clothes. Opulence sets her stage.

Settings are easier to describe than ideas or people, but don't indulge yourself unless you can justify the paycheck.

E X E R C I S E S

- ∽ The major action of my novel takes place in _____ _____.

- ∽ The influence the setting has on the events is _____ _____.

- ∽ The influence the setting has on the characters is _____ _____.

- ∽ To tell my story, for backdrop I will need to describe the scenery:

- ∽ An almost identical story could/could not have occurred in another century, city, on another continent, because _____.

- ∽ The elements of my story derived from a particular time and place are_____. The elements of my story that are universal are _____.

- ∽ To show local color, I will rely on _____.

- ∽ Describe the room or the place where your character works.

- ∽ Describe the room or the place where your character sleeps or makes love.

- ∽ Describe the place your character would go to in his community if he felt like living dangerously.

- ∽ Create the atmosphere your character dwells in by describing conversation taking place in the local coffee shop on Saturday morning which shows ethics, principles, morality, ideas the community believes in or argues about.

- ∽ Re-create the sounds your character hears from her window.

- ∽ It's Sunday morning. Describe the setting where your character spends his time.

- ∽ It's Sunday afternoon. Take your character for a walk. Describe the setting.

- ✪ It's Monday morning. Personify the work environment your character walks into.

- ✪ Describe the ambiance in a setting where your character feels the most tension or pressure.

- ✪ Describe the ambiance in a setting where your character feels the most relaxed.

- ✪ Describe the contents of your character's junk drawer.

- ✪ Describe your character's closet.

- ✪ Create a scene where the natural surroundings change your character's mood.

- ✪ Create a scene with your character looking into a fire on the hearth.

- ✪ Invent a situation in which your character's tidy or messy habits at home, at work, in his car, create a problem with someone else.

- ✪ Personify a place that makes your character anxious.

- ✪ Personify a place that gives your character peace.

- ✪ Show through description your character's taste for quality or tackiness.

- ✪ Your character has a fear of heights. Paint a picture of him on a ladder.

- ✪ Your character is claustrophobic. Paint a picture of him in a stalled elevator.

- ✪ Your character's trailer, apartment, home, etc., is cluttered or has large, open spaces. Describe a scene that shows why he lives in this environment.

- ✪ Your character celebrates an important birthday: 21, 30, 40, 50, 60, 65. She looks back at the important world events she has experienced.

- ✪ List the books and magazines in your character's home.

- ✪ Write a scene in which the weather is the setting.

Wayne's character is angry at the world, especially his world—a small town in North Carolina. He doesn't like the way people overcook green beans, their nosiness, their attitude toward his pot smoking, black people. Doing an exercise above, Wayne sends him back to one place he used to find peace, the old swimming hole. He finds a developer has turned his pastoral playground into rows of ersatz English Tudor houses, where not only do people look into one another's windows, but he can no longer go skinny-dipping. His ranting reveals his insecurities and the unknown aspects of his unhappy childhood.

TIME FRAME

All of the decisions you have been making about your story have contributed to the structure (the way you arrange your plot), but now you are ready to build a frame around your ideas. First you must decide what period of time you will need to tell your tale. When making your decision, don't forget flashbacks, the workhorse in a novelist's stable of techniques. If the story opens when your character is thirty, that doesn't mean you can't include an incident that happened at her high school prom, a friend she lost in kindergarten, or her twenty-first birthday party. Your narrator simply flashes back to the event by saying something like, "Embarrassment was nothing new to Sue. When she was seventeen, shy and overweight, no one had asked her to the senior prom, not even Harold Bromfield. . . ."

For years I have been working on and off on a story set on Memorial Day in a small-town cemetery where everyone comes for a ceremony to honor the dead. Too many characters, living and dead, have worked their way into the plot. The pace is too slow. I'm writing too far away from the action, but when there is world enough and time to concentrate on it again, I have hopes of saving my character from the chatty crowd in the beginning. I'll open with a flashback that will build a bridge or a shortcut to the emotional center of a twenty-year tale revealed on *one* memorable day.

Imagine putting your character on a sailboat with friends or family. You've described a warm day with a good breeze, established the relationships among the characters. Then something goes wrong. The wind dies, or a wildcat storm hits, or a child falls overboard, or another boat hits their craft, or they're beached. You could write an entire novel about what happens during one afternoon. The past would impact on how the characters react under stress, to each other. Their actions would reveal their physical and psychological strengths and weaknesses. According to the viewpoint, you could show how your character felt about herself, how much faith she had, what kind of dreams and fears she harbored.

A common error many beginning writers make is not knowing what to leave out. You need not account for every minute of your character's day. When he wakes up in the morning, don't describe the alarm going off, his brushing his teeth, having breakfast, and picking out a shirt unless one of those acts has significance, like someone having put ground glass in his toothpaste, his eating cold pizza for breakfast showing his indolence, or his wife's having taken her revenge by cutting all the buttons off his shirt. If the previous chapter ended with a dinner party with a client, the next chapter need not open the next day. The next incident can happen ten years later, as long as the reader knows where he is.

Moving from one time period or setting to another can be accomplished with a minimum of fuss, like, "Ten years later, sailing around the world on his boat, Joe didn't even remember the Cleveland client's name."

The technique of moving from one condition, place, or time period to another is called a transition. Critics often pass judgment on novelists for not making smooth passages. If one scene ends with your character interviewing for her first job, and with no indication of the progression of time or events the reader next finds her having a face-lift, your audience feels cheated and confused.

The actual events in James Joyce's *Ulysses* take place in one day. *Gone with the Wind* covers the Civil War and the Reconstruction. *Wuthering Heights* portrays two generations in two families. As in all decisions you make as a novelist, there is no formula, no right or wrong answer to how much time your story covers. But you must decide at what point in time the story opens and where it will end. The time frame will serve you like a jello mold, giving form to your material.

Let's say you decide the action will extend over a week. You could write seven chapters, labeling them for each day of the week, or you could avoid chapter titles but open your story "Monday started out worse than usual . . ." and end with, "Sunday night he wrote his letter of resignation."

At first, writers often ask when to begin and end a new chapter. If you're reading like a writer, you have noticed some novelists write chapters a hundred pages long, while others have ended one before the bottom of a page.

Sometimes a letter, a newspaper article, a page from a diary, will stand alone as a separate chapter.

I think of a chapter like a scene that has a major purpose even though several minor things might also happen while it is being completed. In an earlier section I mentioned creating a minor character who is a clown. I wrote a chapter, told from the viewpoint of the main character, built around the major characters going to watch the clown perform and joining her in a diner after the show. Although the setting changed from Madison Square Garden to a Greenwich Village hangout, the chapter covered the entire evening and was about the protagonist's coming to know the clown by watching her in action and observing the others' responses to her. Each chapter will have a beginning, a middle, and an end, but unlike the structure of a short story or a novel, you must also drop hints, raise questions, create suspicion, about things yet to come. Not every chapter has to end with a cliffhanger, but a good one is a guarantee the reader will turn the page. In my scene at the Greenwich Village hangout, a young man already involved in a long-term relationship with the clown's friend becomes intrigued with the clown. The chapter ends when the naive, trusting friend throws the two together.

In *The Sound and the Fury,* since Faulkner jumped all over the place in terms of time, place, and narration, he dated the four sections of his novel: April Seventh, 1928; June Second, 1910; April Sixth, 1928; April Eighth, 1928.

E X E R C I S E S

- ⋙ My novel opens on _____ (month, day, year) at _____ o'clock, when my character is _____ years old.

- ⋙ My novel ends on _____, when my character is _____.

- ⋙ The time frame for my story is in the past. It happened _____ (days, weeks, years) ago, or I am telling it as if _____ is the present and the reader is experiencing the events as they happen to my character.

- ∽ I will use flashbacks to cover significant events that took place when she was _____.

- ∽ Your last scene was set at lunch. Write a transition that moves your character ahead one week.

- ∽ Your character is talking to a friend. Write the transition for a flashback to his childhood.

- ∽ Write a sentence that will bring your character back from the childhood story to the present.

- ∽ The crucial event, the epiphany, the important decision for my character, happens when _____. My story opens on the day it occurs, a year later, two weeks before, as it is taking place.

- ∽ The important historical events (wars, Presidents' terms, social issues such as civil rights, the abortion controversy, Supreme Court appointments, the economy, riots, foreign affairs) that happened during the time frame of my story are _____. They do/do not have significance in my plot.

Marc's yuppie lawyer is fired (the crucial event) in the first chapter. The rest of the novel (his epiphany) deals with the effect.

CONFLICT

Conflict is trouble. Without trouble, there is no story. If Iago had been a devoted subordinate, we would never have heard of Othello and Desdemona. If Othello had not had a possessive nature, "I loved not wisely, but too well" would not have become the classic jealous lover's excuse.

The struggle growing out of the interplay of opposing forces creates interest and suspense. The opposing forces can be your character against nature—fire, flood, earthquake, drought; against fate—the cards are stacked against him by seemingly uncontrollable forces; against an enemy—an antagonist who is his boss, his brother; against society—a poor Hispanic girl trying to be accepted as a scholarship student at Smith; against evil—a detective, sheriff, soldier, trying to restore order to a community or a country besieged by crooks or killers; against conflicting aspects of his own character—

he is a greedy materialist but wants to be an artist, or he wants power, but he's a coward.

Conflict is the friction, struggle, dissension, controversy your character experiences that forces his actions and creates tension in your story. Remember, every story must have one/some problem to stand between him and what he wants most. It can be opposing forces within his own nature, family, or society, or the tussle can be between him and an antagonist, an actual opponent, as stated above, or the adversary can be effective because he appeals to a flaw or a weakness in the protagonist's character as Iago appeals to Othello's jealousy. In highly competitive companies, Faust might be able to make a trade for power. On many mean streets, dressed like a drug dealer, he finds money will make the deal. Some parents would sell their souls for the love of their contentious children.

If your plot depends upon an adversary, develop your bad guy with as much care as you do the protagonist. As John Milton taught us with his captivating Devil in *Paradise Lost,* the antagonist can run away with your story, especially for American readers. Don't forget, we inherited our myths and values from a group of rebels defying the law and order of the Crown. Our mythical heroes are cowboys, who rode away from culture, convention, and civilization until they ran out of wilderness. Many people read to pretend for a few hours they have the courage, the gumption, to defy the rules as the Godfather does. As our voting patterns indicate, we often identify with the underdog. In the mystery and suspense genres, devotees demand to understand what motivates the deviant. Hack writers often take a shortcut, writing off the villain simply as disturbed, but the good scoundrel is complex, like Hannibal Lecter in *Silence of the Lambs.*

If your story is to have serious meaning and profound consequences, the foe or other forces must attack your character from the inside as well as the outside. The reader must see him make moral choices, deal with difficult dilemmas. To get the job, he must betray his friend; to obey his commander, he must kill innocent people; to have the woman he loves, he must leave his wife and child; to solve the crime/do his duty, he must defeat someone he comes to respect; to win, he must deny his deepest beliefs; to find happiness, she must shirk her responsibility. Faulkner said all meaning in the best fiction comes from the heart in conflict with itself.

Think of conflict this way. Your character wants or needs something, such as power, revenge, a woman, a child, a violin, to play for the Yankees. In an intriguing story, circumstances or other characters intervene. What barriers stand between your character and his desire? Or perhaps he has lost something—dignity, self-respect, reputation, love, success, money, the game, his marbles. What opposition will he encounter in trying to regain what he has lost? Will the hindrance be internal, external, or both?

Your task will be to create a conflict to grip your reader either because she cares about the character and wants her to triumph, like Hardy's Tess of the D'Urbervilles, or because she finds the struggle fascinating. The reader must care about how it turns out. Ahab wasn't a likeable character, but why a man is willing to sacrifice himself and his crew to destroy a whale is intriguing.

In John Knowles's *A Separate Peace,* for fifteen years a man, presented as a decent type, has been troubled by a tragic event that happened when he was in prep school. He might have been responsible for the accident that killed his best friend. The story opens with his returning to the school to solve the puzzle. Did he do it? If he did, why did he do it? Was his friend Finney actually his antagonist? The story, told in flashback, is a man's journey to self-discovery, to understanding the conflict within himself, and finally, to forgiveness.

In the workshop, Heather's character and Chip's are gay, but the conflict is different. Heather's Andy is quite comfortable with her sexual orientation. In Madison, Wisconsin, she has a set of friends who support her lifestyle. It's her choice of childish, needy, not-always-trustworthy Sue as a lover that has caused the problem. Grey, Chip's protagonist, is married, has a mortgage, two children, a nice dog, a difficult live-in mother, and an unsatisfied nature not caused by the mortgage or the difficult mother. His conflict is internal, his inability to recognize and accept his homosexuality. Chip's challenge is to create dramatic irony, wherein the reader realizes what Grey is avoiding before he does, while still making this character credible and sympathetic.

The problem created by the conflict has to be resolved. Your character can win, lose, die, or walk away from the problem, but something has to have changed. Although some very effective stories—like Arthur Miller's play *Death of a Salesman,* and Willa Cather's short story "Paul's Case"—have ended in successfully motivated suicides, killing off your character in frustration because you can't settle the conflict is not a terrific idea.

Let's say your character has lost something. Ask yourself questions such as these: Can he find it again? Can he live without it? What will have to happen for him to obtain it? Will he have to change? Is his changing possible? Will it take a miracle or a Hollywood scriptwriter? Working through these exercises helps not only to understand the conflict, but also to develop the character and structure the story.

The following exercises could be the first step in determining the main conflict in your story. After you have found one that gives you ideas for developing your plot, finding the essence of your character, put it under your mind's microscope. If no one trusts him, why don't they? What has he done in the past to lose their faith? If he has done something questionable or that he regrets, what motivated his behavior? Was he guilty of misconduct or falsely accused? What can he do to regain confidence? Is he capable of doing what must be done, or of clearing his name? Whom can he count on? What are the hurdles?

EXERCISES

∞ My character's worst enemy is:

himself	another person	his family's expectations
bad luck	society's disdain	an animal
his temper	his appearance	his anger

his lack of:

funds	direction	intelligence
skills	humor	imagination
drive	education	friends
talent	contacts	heart

∞ The story is primarily about her dream, her regret, her loss, her battle, her success, her failure, her search, her family ties, _____ .

∞ WHAT IF her nemesis were a myth?

- WHAT IF he blamed the wrong person?
- WHAT IF she lost her eyesight?
- WHAT IF he had to choose between her and his family?
- WHAT IF she had to break a serious promise?
- WHAT IF no one would trust him?
- WHAT IF none of her friends liked him?
- WHAT IF he were jealous of his brother?
- WHAT IF she intimidated men?
- WHAT IF he envied his wife?
- WHAT IF she were in love with her stepfather?
- WHAT IF it meant she would get the kids?
- WHAT IF he were impotent?
- WHAT IF she were sterile?
- WHAT IF he were an alcoholic?
- WHAT IF they had become enemies in high school?
- WHAT IF he beat her sister?
- WHAT IF her need to be loved overshadowed her judgment?
- WHAT IF he were the only Mexican in his office?
- WHAT IF she were the only gay in her town/her family?
- WHAT IF he had the feelings, but not the words?
- WHAT IF she didn't have the confidence to manage her staff, discipline her children?
- WHAT IF he couldn't handle her success?
- WHAT IF she had the drive, but hadn't realized she didn't have the skill or the talent?
- WHAT IF he were haughty?
- WHAT IF she were proud?
- WHAT IF he blamed everyone and everything except himself?
- WHAT IF her child were diagnosed as a manic-depressive?
- WHAT IF he couldn't overcome the self-image he had accepted as a child?
- WHAT IF she had a clever enemy at work who managed to hide his dirty deeds?
- WHAT IF she had damaging evidence about a superior that

could bring him down, but she wasn't certain she could trust
the person to whom her superior reported?

    ∞ WHAT IF he couldn't live down his family's reputation?

    ∞ WHAT IF she had a history of falling for the wrong guy?

    ∞ WHAT IF he had managed to hide the fact he had done
hard time?

    ∞ WHAT IF, to get her divorced father's attention, she acted
out in ways that only widened the gap?

    ∞ WHAT IF he felt he had married beneath his station?

    ∞ WHAT IF she felt he hadn't grown and developed in the areas
that were important to her?

    ∞ WHAT IF a father with tastes for Shakespeare, Schubert, and
sherry raised a daughter who preferred beer, bikes, and
break dancing?

    ∞ WHAT IF he could not find a spot in the world where his
heart and head would work in harmony?

    ∞ WHAT IF she had called in all of her chits and was still in
trouble?

An important element of suspense in Alice's story was who
had been plagiarizing Lucian's work. Doing the exercise about
a clever enemy at work, she shrieked, "It was Xenophone!!!"
The others in the workshop, who adored the cynical slave,
screamed in protest and disbelief—just the response she was
after, of course.

THE CLIMAX

At this stage, you should feel great. Look at the tough decisions you've made about your story. It's as if you've been
arduously putting together a puzzle. Now the picture is beginning to emerge, but one important piece, the climax, is missing. You have created this absorbing character, concocted a
mess, and plunked him into the middle of it. Now it's time to
decide when, where, how, or if it is possible to get him out
of it.

The climax is the point of highest interest in a story, the
place where you are asking the reader to make his greatest
emotional response. At the climax, the murder is solved, the

main character changes, she makes an important decision, faces someone or something, charts a new course, wins, loses, says the hell with it and gives up.

All of us have seen those neat triangles in textbooks—a straight line, labeled "rising action," to the climax with the opposite side marked "falling action." Let me warn you, it's easier to draw the figure than to plot a novel so perfectly. My professors declared Hawthorne got it exactly right in *The Scarlet Letter*. Later, I intimidated my students with *The Great Gatsby*, every teacher's dream for demonstrating structure. I have had kind students. Not one of them ever asked me to try to fit *Gravity's Rainbow* on that tidy triangle.

In *The Art of Fiction*, John Gardner drew a modified version of the testy triangle I find more helpful for beginning writers. The rising action makes several dips, showing those episodes leading to minor climaxes, which create the suspense, fascination, and anxiety, feelings that keep the readers turning the pages before they reach the major climax.

Think of stories connecting a beginning and an end across a field of strong forces.

To illustrate the point, we will create a dramatic situation. The backstory: ambitious and intelligent, Hetty, a partner in a prestigious and conservative Park Avenue law firm, had always known she was adopted. Fortunately, she loved the politically moderate family who had raised her. Even though they had told her if she ever wanted to know who her birth parents were, they would help her find them, she had not been moved to trace her heritage. In law school, Hetty had married Morgan, a law student from a conservative New England family. She managed to have an acceptable, if not affectionate, relationship with her straitlaced in-laws, even though their social and political ideas were too far to the right for her more pragmatic stance.

The story opens when the couple are in their late thirties. Morgan is being courted to run for political office against the liberal Democratic incumbent, they are financially secure, and as a partner in the international division of her firm, Hetty knows her career is safe if she stays the course. She decides to have a baby. Hetty is surprised but delighted by how thrilled she is about having the child. Soon after she is pregnant, although Morgan and his family try to discourage her, she decides if she's ever going to locate her real parents, this is the time to do it. With her adoptive mother's help, she discovers an eighteen-year-old, unmarried woman named Mary Myrna Betts had given birth to Hetty in Raleigh, North Carolina, thirty-nine years earlier. Although they make an effort, Hetty and Mary Myrna do not bond. Mary Myrna feels Hetty is an elitist snob who looks down on her. Hetty thinks her birth mother gives up too easily. As Hetty starts to leave, already having decided this would be her only visit, Mary Myrna says, "That boy I told you about who knocked me up? His daddy was black."

The climax of the story a writer would build toward is Hetty's decision. Does she tell Morgan? Her biased in-laws? Her conservative partners? Does she have an abortion? What happens as a result of her decision is the falling action, or conclusion. Readers will keep turning the pages to find out what happens, but the challenge to the writer is to build the anxiety until they are holding their breath in anticipation of what Hetty decides to do. For the reader to care enough to be predicting what Hetty decides, the author will have had to create many dips—building to minor climaxes along the way that will affect or add to the difficulty of making the decision. Tense situations with her in-laws, tight spots for her husband's political career, dilemmas in her firm, difficulty in conceiving the child, will add to the tension of her making a choice that will affect everything and reveal if she is wise, courageous, made from stern stuff.

As the author, you arrange a series of episodes like Hetty's, motivated by character and situation, to build and sustain tension and interest on the way to the high point, the climax. All of the other trials have intensified the importance of this scene.

Warning: if, when your character faces predicaments, you have no doubt he would always do the honorable/dishonorable thing, you probably do not know him and his situation well enough to tell his story. Abraham Lincoln suffered from melancholia. Al Capone loved his mother. Remember, one calm summer night Richard Cory "went home and put a bullet through his head." Think of the moments a nice person like you has wished someone would die; or you've cheated, lied; or those times when someone you considered self-absorbed did something extraordinary, like staying up all night to console a friend or giving money he couldn't afford to help Rumanian orphans. Why did you do those things, have those thoughts? Why does your character?

Predictability is the serial killer of fine fiction. If the reader has figured out what Hetty will do before she does it, why should he keep turning the pages?

He probably won't have to. Predictability bores agents and editors too. In my opinion, Hardy's *Jude the Obscure* is the most unpredictable novel in Western culture. I reread it every three or four years, hoping this time it will turn out differently, in a way that doesn't hurt so bad. The challenge for storytellers, of course, is to create "not what you expect" and to make it credible.

An interesting, "not what you expect" episode in Mary Gordon's novella "Immaculate Man" (*The Rest of Life*) entails a middle-aged woman falling in love with a forty-three-year-old man, but he is the virgin. Readers not totally jaded will find the situation credible because he is a priest.

Writers in the workshop often justify an incredible passage with a fact-is-stranger-than-fiction defense by saying, "But this really happened." I no longer recall what wise person said, "Fiction is obliged to stick to possibility; truth is not," but I use it often.

No matter how well you know your character and her story, be prepared for the unplanned twists and turns your plot could take. Characters have a way of taking on minds of their own and leading you down interesting and significant detours. They are also apt to encounter a minor character who was meant to have a walk-on part but becomes the man who came to dinner. Be flexible to new ideas and inspirations.

When structuring your story, keep in mind this is not a geometry course. You don't have to follow a formula to find the answer. You could decide to open with the climax, building backward to explain the enticing beginning when Mary Myrna says, "That boy I told you about who knocked me up? His daddy was black." Readers are more apt to be interested in *how* and *why* something happened rather than *what* happened.

E X E R C I S E S

- ⭇ The most important decision my character will make is _____.

- ⭇ My character has a significant choice to make that involves _____.

- ∞ The high point of my story will come when my character realizes _____.

- ∞ The aspect of my character's personality that will make it difficult for her to decide, make a choice, examine her life, is _____.

- ∞ Several possible ways I might resolve my character's conflict are:

- ∞ Because of his nature, my story will be more credible if I choose _____.

- ∞ To avoid giving away what happens too soon, I will keep the reader guessing by _____.

- ∞ What prevents my character from resolving the conflict in the way the reader will "wish it were" is _____ _____. Or because of my character's _____, it would be inconceivable for her conflict not to be resolved in her favor.

- ∞ The climax of my novel will be reached when _____ _____ happens.

- ∞ The actual scene will take place in my character's head, a hotel room, during a telephone conversation, when someone reads a letter, when she quits, when she signs on the dotted line, after an accident on a foggy night, when he pulls the trigger, when he feels the cuffs click, when the child falls off the horse, _____.

- ∞ I plan for this to happen early on, approximately at the midpoint of my yarn, in the opening sentence, on the last page, or _____.

- ∞ At this point, I know of (three, six, ten) _____ _____ crises or episodes that will occur on my character's way to resolving the conflict, which are _____.

Steve's story opens with a murder. His colleagues in the workshop assume the climax will come when his protagonist, a burned-out lawyer, proves his young client—accused of killing his girlfriend—is innocent, or he is convicted. But the story takes on added depth when the case rekindles the lawyer's spirit. The emotional high point comes when he makes important decisions in his own life.

THEME

When Bill Clinton ran for President, the theme of his campaign was change. This abstract concept was the nucleus of every speech and the core of answers he gave to voters and the media. The President's change doctrine or thesis worked like a clothesline to which he could attach his ideas about taxes, health care, civil rights.

In music the melody is the theme. Those recurring patterns of notes set the mood and the tone of the piece.

The theme of a novel is what it means. Your story might be about a good man who becomes a good minister. Your preacher has such a talent for delivering sermons, the congregation flatters and rewards him excessively, until he begins to believe he is God. The theme, simplified, is "power corrupts."

John Milton's theme for *Paradise Lost* was to justify God's ways to man. In a letter, Jane Austen said the theme of *Mansfield Park* was ordination. Some critics say the theme of Conrad's *Heart of Darkness* is man's fascination with abomination or evil.

Biblical themes, like the cleansing power of charity, often underlie the toughest of stories, but a theme is not a moral. Rather, a theme explores the emotional experience of the principle of right and wrong.

Think of a theme as an investigation of an idea like lust that leads to love, marriage as doom or ruin, evil's craving to devour good, politics becoming a religion, an eye for an eye, despair as a sin. Your duty as a novelist is not to solve the puzzle, create a law, but to speculate, propose, suppose, suggest this is the way it could happen to these people at this time.

Don't throw away your notebook if you have a character and a story but don't yet feel ready to dazzle anyone with a brilliant motif that explains the essence of your plot. There are writers who start with an idea like serving a higher truth than civil authority, as Sophocles must have when he created *Antigone*. But more often you will discover the meaning or the theme as your character begins to tell you his story, especially if you remember to ask him not only "And then what happened? " but WHY it happened.

Some people confess they don't find their themes until they

have finished their first drafts. If that's the way it goes with your story, the discovery will help you make corrections, such as eliminating incidents or scenes that don't contribute to your central idea. Look at the following to help focus your thoughts.

E X E R C I S E S

- ∽ I am most interested in examining what heals, hurts, or destroys my character.

- ∽ Issues that intrigue me are the effects on the human condition of race, isolation, money, power, human cruelty, indifference, pomposity, religion, or _____.

- ∽ My character's interest in _____, obsession with _____, fear of _____ _____, love for _____ _____, could lead me to explore ideas such as _____.

- ∽ The theme for my novel could grow out of:

  • My character's head and heart are in discord over _____ _____.

  • My character is in conflict with _____ _____.

  • My character becomes passionate about _____ _____.

  • My character becomes hysterical about _____ _____.

  • My character feels harassed by _____ _____.

  • My character hates _____, loves _____ _____, feels guilty about _____ _____.

  • My character would go to the barricades for _____ _____.

- ∽ Social or moral issues I think could be dramatized to support my theme (not treated as propaganda) are: _____ _____.

The group admired Jim's courage but were skeptical when he turned up in the workshop saying he would write from the viewpoint of a young woman. But his charming, manipulative Tracy captivated them immediately. Deception was his theme. As Tracy skillfully deceived everyone, and always herself, the other writers squirmed. The universality of Jim's motif gave them insights that were occasionally uncomfortable.

STRUCTURE:
THE BEGINNING, THE MIDDLE, THE END

Early on, I suggested you not waste time making an elaborate outline but begin writing your novel when you know the last line. That is still my theory, even though I'm about to devote an entire section to proposing you think about and work on structure. The advice is not contradictory, although at first brush, it might seem so. The decisions you have been making about your story—the setting, the time frame, the theme— have already begun to build a structure.

Finding a character is finding the life force of your novel. She comes with a story running through her bloodstream. I've never met a writer who said only his character is a woman with a long black braid. He says she's twenty-seven, has unfortunate taste in men, runs a ragtag airport—unprofitably—on a grassy strip in Maine, and is stubborn as a mule. After doing some exercises to give his imagination a jump start, becoming a method actor who walks around in her shoes with a notebook in his pocket, he discovers her name is Frankie. A Boston cartel, using unsavory means, is trying to buy or force her out. Her own pride and tenacity, that won't let her admit when she's made a mistake, create as many problems as the syndicate.

When the writer decides the last line is, "That spring Frankie planted sunflowers on the airstrip," or, "When they pinned commercial copilot wings on Frankie's uniform, she was digging her nails into her palm," or, "No one was really surprised when Frankie was the one who played kamikaze over her own strip," he is ready to start his first draft, even if he hasn't created all the crises, complications, and conflicts of the heart she will experience before arriving at the conclusion.

Anyone who has spent any time in a schoolhouse knows a

story has a beginning, a middle, and an end, known in literary terms as the *exposition*, *the development* (or Aristotle's more descriptive term, *complication*), and the *denouement*. Wouldn't it be neat and tidy if you could plan to divide your three-hundred-page story into three exact parts, knowing on page 100 you had completed the exposition or introduction and now could begin to build the complications to page 200, where you would reach the climax with one hundred pages left to tie up the loose ends and write a moving but satisfying conclusion? Unfortunately, many unruly stories won't comply. Besides, your devoting a hundred pages to the introduction would be as effective as a door-to-door salesman's spending an hour introducing himself before he tried to sell his product. The reader would slam the door.

Exposition

The exposition introduces the character, creates the tone, gives the setting, reveals the viewpoint, and supplies other facts necessary to understanding the story. Our writer above has already wisely decided not to start with Frankie's birth, but to introduce her when she is twenty-seven years old, running the airstrip in Maine. He can easily *show* us the problem with the cartel by creating an early action scene where the members put pressure on her to sell, vandalize her equipment, etc., or he can expose the problem through dialogue between Frankie and a worker, friend, cousin, etc. Normally, the least effective way would be for the narrator to state the problem in a flat-footed way. However, the writer may choose to tell, rather than show, if he wants to underplay the syndicate's role and establish the fact Frankie's nature causes her more trouble than a herd of charging bulls or disreputable Boston businessmen could create. Saying she has too much pride won't do. The reader will have to see her lose something or someone she wants desperately rather than ask for or accept help that may have given her the prize, or he will have to watch her arrogance force her to make a bad choice, like putting herself or others in harm's way.

If the writer decides to tell Frankie's story chronologically, he will have to rely on flashbacks to give us her backstory—showing how life experience or her genes have made her bullheaded, and often ruled by pride rather than by good sense. The reader will also need to know how she came to own the strip, why the Boston group wants it, why she is attracted to yet another man others see as an unfortunate choice. But the writer is not compelled—is advised not—to give all the information in one chunk, which would slow down the pacing. Pages of straight facts with no action or dialogue would be as interesting as reading a stack of résumés. Also, I have worked with beginning writers who made the mistake of summarizing their entire story in the first chapter, leaving them with no surprises and little means of intriguing their readers. Intersperse the information the reader needs to know into dialogue and action of the ongoing story, like a red thread occasionally woven into a piece of cloth.

Remember, you are like the old, oral storyteller sitting around a campfire, entertaining, enlightening, stirring, and from the moment you say, "Once upon a time . . ." always working to hold the listeners' attention. Early on, they have to like or be interested enough in your character to care what happens to her. Frankie can exasperate them until they want to shake her, but they also have to see her charm, identify with, or at least understand, her internal conflicts. You will want them to see her as a credible person who might live next door, or as someone who is fascinating, or who makes them secretly envious of her bizarre behavior they would never have the nerve to try.

Your characters will be more sympathetic if the suspense depends more on emotion than on events. When done well, conflicts of the heart can grip a reader more than murder or mayhem.

In our workshop, one of the funniest, most touching, tense, and ironic scenes took place in a seemingly simple situation. Gillian's character Marya, a young lawyer under an extreme time bind in her firm, was pressured into shopping for a bathing suit in a busy department store with her domineering mother and her mother's bossy friend, Sylvia. We felt Marya's acute embarrassment and repressed fury as the older women took command of the swimsuit department. When they bellowed critical remarks about her anatomy, we sensed order at Lord & Taylor was about to be disrupted. Would Marya finally blow, hurling bikinis, breaking mirrors and the controlling tie with her mother? Would the salesclerks and customers turn on the overbearing women, pelting them with their purses and pencils? What reader couldn't sympathize with a character whose mother poked her fingers between the elastic and her daughter's leg in an attempt to push un-wanted flesh out of sight? In a short scene, Gillian managed to use broad hips as a means of exposing tensions on a multi-tude of levels, ranging from the dilemma career women face between childbearing and their careers to mothers' expecta-tions and daughters' dreams. In an interesting, not-what-you-expect twist, the daughter has the maternal instinct, the mother the fierce need for her daughter to be a success.

In the beginning of your story, you are trying to introduce your reader to a character who—broad hips, flaws, and all—will become a friend. Think about how you have grown to care about someone. What first captured your attention? What did you want to know about this person? What did he do to reveal who he was inside the suit? What made you uncomfortable? How did you learn more and more about his background? Use it.

The usual opening of a novel is disruption of order. I'm not suggesting you must begin with an earthquake, a chase, or the arrival of an alien. The engine in Frankie's plane won't turn over. Your character is perplexed, sad, confused, angry, ashamed. The weather is bad, the dog got run over, her hus-band got drunk, her daughter got expelled, she got fired, he fell for someone else, a check bounced, his proposal was re-jected, ants are living in the sugar, someone laughed. If every-thing is already hunky-dory, the reader will have no reason to read on. She knows stories, like life, are about trouble and problems that must be resolved. Those ants could be a sym-bol of other things that are devouring the sweetness in the character's life, or the character could be too stressed to keep her life or her kitchen clean, or . . .

Page 1, even if it's a page of description, raises questions, suspicions, and expectations; the mind casts forward to later pages, wondering what will come and how.

E X E R C I S E S

- ❧ The first impression I want the reader to have of my character is _____.

- ❧ To create that impression (her humor, beauty, cynicism, cow-ardliness, confusion, stuffiness, poverty, intelligence), I will in-

troduce her doing _____ or saying
_____, or the narrator will set the tone
by _____.

∽ The disorder that will open my novel is _____
_____.

∽ If it is important for the reader to know immediately the setting—time, place, ambiance—I will show the backdrop
by _____.

∽ My reader will need to know the following things that happened before the story opens:

∽ I can use the following from that backstory to create the
unexpected:

∽ I want my reader to realize the major conflict immediately, or
I will reveal it slowly because _____.

∽ To set up my story, in addition to the protagonist I must
introduce my reader to another character or characters. I need
to bring them immediately to the forefront, showing how
they interact with my character—or would it be more effective
for my character to whet the reader's appetite by talking,
thinking, or hearing about them before they appear?

∽ The question I will pose early to create suspense, tension, or
suspicion is _____.

Earlier, I mentioned Maria's Blackstone, the corrupt politician who begins his day (and her novel) wondering who he
can fuck that day. He is shaving, which gives her an opportunity to describe him physically. His musings into the mirror
allow her to explain what he does for a living and where he
commits his dirty deeds. In one short paragraph she has established a tone, setting, good-versus-evil theme, and although readers will realize they should hope he cuts his
throat with the razor, they won't. Blackstone intrigues them.
They want to know more.

The Development, Complication, or Rising Action

The development, complication, or rising action is the portion of the plot that complicates the action by increasing the
tension, intrigue, or trepidation, making the reader want to
know how the story is going to turn out. This is the place for
the dips in the rising action. If you know your character well,

this is the easiest and the most fun part to write. Your job is to create episodes showing forces that work against your character's will and those that support her.

Some of the most beguiling and revealing scenes in literature occur in a character's mind when he takes the reader into his confidence. No one else is around, so he divulges feelings and ideas he would never expose publicly.

A combination of scenes nudged forward by thoughts, events, situations, and connections with other people works best. In the proposed story above, Frankie can't meet her payroll, and her mechanic's pregnant wife gives birth to a premature baby. Instead of trying to persuade Frankie to sell the airstrip, the acquisitions manager for the cartel works on her guilt by talking about the morality of employer responsibility to his workers. Frankie's spunk, pride, recklessness, and/or desperation give her the guts to enter a dangerous stunt show for prize money. Her engine stalls. . . .

Those of you reading and working from this book, people who like to tell stories, can spin out dozens of these episodes, but rein in for a moment. You will concentrate on the plot later. You have already thought about theme or the significance of your story, but, of course, it can't really be separated from structure. The theme unifies the plot. If the structure is the skeleton, the theme is the backbone. An ear or a nose won't work on a spine any better than an episode unrelated to your theme will fit your plot—no matter how interesting or well shaped or beautifully written it may be. You will know you are a serious writer when you can punch "Delete" for a scene you love, but can't justify what it does to reveal your character or advance your plot.

If you like to describe a crashing surf on a lonely beach but your story is about Ken Krug, who has been landlocked in Kansas since birth, instead of sticking on a scene that would be as fitting as a ruffle on a rug, write a letter to Aunt Sally about the crashing surf. Keep Ken Krug plodding the plains.

In this development portion of the story, your character, just as a friend does, sometimes charms, disappoints, delights, does silly things, makes you impatient, uses bad judgment, and arrives at ridiculous decisions. Funny, interesting, sad, embarrassing, pathetic, ironic, troubling, surprising things happen to your character on her way up the hill to the climax. All of these incidents have significance and meaning. They will determine if she captures the gold ring, has failed dreams or false aspirations.

In a plot, stock situations—often-used sequences of action—are the counterpart to stock characters discussed earlier. You could probably list a hundred boy-meets-girl plots, but think of the differences. The glass slipper doesn't always fit. The rags-to-riches-by-pluck-and-luck plot made popular by Horatio Alger is often the basis for zippy reads, but not always credible novels, by authors like Jackie Collins and Sidney Sheldon, etc., but literary writers such as Theodore Dreiser and Sinclair Lewis have done variations on the storyline. Even Emily Brontë's Heathcliff could fit into the category. So don't hesitate to build your story on plot ideas exploited many times before. You won't be plagiarizing. There is no way you can see the world or write like anyone else except yourself.

E X E R C I S E S

- ∞ The weakness in my character's personality that will hinder him is _____.

- ∞ Incidents, scenes, crises that will reveal the flaw in her character are _____.

- ∞ The person or persons who will play on his weakness are _____.

- ∞ I will reveal how the adversary works by showing her doing, or saying, or thinking _____.

- ∞ My character's support will come from his ability to _____.

- ∞ The other characters who will help her, give her encouragement, care about her, are _____.

- ∞ They will show their support when _____ _____ happens, or by telling _____.
_____.

- ∞ The social element she moves in will help or hinder my character by _____.

- ∽ My character will/will not be able to count on his family or his heritage. I will reveal the backing he does or does not receive by _____.

- ∽ A REVIEW:
  - The big question or problem to be resolved in my story is _____.
  - The major obstacle is _____.
  - The scene where the quandary will be answered is _____.
  - Some of the complications my character will experience trying to solve the dilemma are _____.

- ∽ WHAT IF an unknown relative turned up?

- ∽ WHAT IF her parents said she was too good for him?

- ∽ WHAT IF he received a postcard that changed things?

- ∽ WHAT IF he insisted she convert?

- ∽ WHAT IF a shady deal came along?

- ∽ WHAT IF the child was born handicapped?

- ∽ WHAT IF she loved the guy but hated the ring?

- ∽ WHAT IF they said she was too old?

- ∽ WHAT IF, when it was time to move, he arranged a business trip?

- ∽ WHAT IF he had enjoyed the courses in school but found he hated being an accountant, a lawyer, a pediatrician, a traveling salesman?

- ∽ WHAT IF she said she had fallen in love with another woman?

- ∽ WHAT IF he expected her to take a backseat?

- ∽ WHAT IF she appeared at the back door and wouldn't leave?

- ∽ WHAT IF he picked out the house without her?

- ∽ WHAT IF the self-deprecation was a cover for her feeling superior?

- ∽ WHAT IF he kept building her up, then letting her down?

- ∽ WHAT IF she was a confronter, and he couldn't handle conflict?

- ∽ WHAT IF everyone else knew he was after her money?

- ∽ WHAT IF the child insisted he had molested her?

- ∽ WHAT IF she couldn't be herself and succeed?

- ∞ WHAT IF he finally came to realize what was missing in his life?

- ∞ WHAT IF she couldn't handle the loneliness?

- ∞ WHAT IF he realized she stayed with him only because of financial fears?

- ∞ WHAT IF she knew he came back only because he couldn't support two households?

- ∞ WHAT IF her child was the only one who wouldn't forgive her?

- ∞ WHAT IF being his mother's favorite had been the curse of his life?

- ∞ WHAT IF her father died never having told her he loved her?

- ∞ WHAT IF his aunt tried to alienate him from his mother?

- ∞ WHAT IF she learned something devastating about her boss?

- ∞ WHAT IF he had been the middle child?

- ∞ WHAT IF she had been the firstborn?

An exercise about the postcard grew into a key element in Wayne's plot when his character began to receive cards, always with a white horse on the front (which made him swear under his breath). The cards were signed "Amelia," whom he claimed not to know, but his wife thought there was another woman. The significance of the horse and who Amelia really was added suspense and tension for several chapters.

The Denouement, Falling Action, Conclusion

The final section of your novel is the resolution of the story. Denouement, falling action, and conclusion are literary synonyms for the resolution. The ending is too narrow a definition for denouement, falling action, or conclusion, which is the unknotting of the plot after the conflict has been resolved.

As we will discuss in more detail later, all plotting is cause and effect. What happens when the conflict is resolved is the cause for what happens in the denouement. When Hamlet finally overcomes his doubts and conscience and decides to kill Claudius, the effect is the duel which ends in the death of Hamlet, Laertes, Claudius, and Gertrude. In our hypothetical story above, if Frankie decides to maintain her independence and not take on a partner who has capital, the effect could be the loss of her airstrip and her autonomous lifestyle. What effect the decision or event has and what it means are the final questions to answer for your reader in the denouement.

This section is the fulfillment of a promise. You will satisfy the reader's curiosity, answer all questions. The action or intrigue ends in success or failure, or the mystery is solved, or the misunderstanding is cleared away, or the character pays the price for her decisions. The denouement sometimes involves the discovery or disclosure of an important fact hitherto unknown to a character, such as Frankie's discovering the man she has cared about was working for the syndicate all along, or Hetty's learning that her birth mother was lying all along.

The falling action can include a reversal of your character's fortune, his destruction, or his success—Hamlet is killed in the duel; Moby Dick and Ishmael win, but Ahab loses; Hetty comes to understand, even though she does not have a black heritage, she can't stay married to a man whose prejudiced views are stronger than his love for her; Frankie realizes her own arrogance caused her to lose what she prizes most.

However, the denouement is not only the outcome of the main situation, but also an explanation of all the secrets and misunderstandings connected with the plot complications. Your story might involve reuniting characters, clearing up mistaken identity, explaining misunderstood intentions or motivations, discovering dirty tricks.

Writers find pleasure in creating a good sentence, in finding the right word, but when you hear them talking about writing for the pure joy of it, many are talking about the reward they realize in working out the denouement. The struggle, the thought, the brooding over their characters, the effort they have put into capturing reality in words, images, actions, and symbols, have paid off with more significance than they had imagined.

Here is where you will come to understand the relationships of all the elements in your plot. Some readers' pleasure will end with emotional, if not intellectual, perception, but for them to have either experience, you—the writer—must have found a deeper level of meaning than you understood when you began. Don't fret if you haven't yet had a grand epiphany. You haven't done anything wrong. When you begin, there is no way to plan for symbolic significance of events, subtle connections, reoccurring images that will creep into your work and have consequences. Much of it will occur as you begin to dig deeper into your character's psyche, or will come from your subconscious.

How do you make the discoveries that will enrich your denouement? At this point, reading your entire manuscript over and over will not be procrastination. You are looking for clues, symbols, images, metaphors, repetitions, and are probing for their meaning, perhaps strengthening them. The denouement is where you will unify the plot. Rereading what you have done will help you not only to find another level of meaning, but also to tighten your story. Now is the time for discovering extraneous aspects that lead nowhere, accomplish nothing. If you have a scene, dialogue, or incident that has no relevance as to how you are going to wind up your story or what it means, get rid of it.

Look at the order of the scenes to determine if there is a logical building to the result you are now planning. If people behaved the way your character did, is this what would have happened? Have you made the outcome too predictable? Is there still enough intrigue left for readers to be interested in how the story turns out and what it means?

Perhaps you haven't asked yourself all the questions that could add depth to your story. For weeks I've been working on a story about my protagonist's intimate relationship with a well-known writer who begins to lose touch with reality. Halfway through the story, which lacked something, it dawned on me I had concentrated on her feelings toward him but had looked only superficially at his perspective of her. Now I'll go around bumping into walls, lightposts, and parking meters, asking myself, "What did she mean to him?" and "Why did he feel that way?" The story will still be told from her point of view, but I'll have important information to work into my plot.

E X E R C I S E S

- The things in my story the reader still does not know are _____.

- I will tie up those loose ends by _____.

∝ The relationships of characters to be resolved are _____
_____.

∝ The reader will be surprised to learn _____
_____.

∝ The misunderstanding I must clear away is _____
_____.

∝ The price my character pays for her decisions is _____
_____.

∝ The reward my character receives for her actions is _____
_____.

∝ The ending of my story will be a result of fate, traits of my character's nature, a dramatic event, or _____
_____.

Heather cleverly manages to conclude her story with a dilemma resulting from a combination of fate, her character's nature, and a dramatic event. Childish and irresponsible Sue, Andy's lesbian lover, gets pregnant and wants to have an abortion. Sensible and reliable Andy not only forgives her infidelity, but wants them to raise the baby. Andy convinces the reader she would be a terrific parent. This might be her only opportunity, but then she's stuck with Sue, who everyone realizes is the wrong mate for Andy, such an appealing character. The group in Heather's workshop could never agree on how they wanted the story to end.

CHAPTER 10

Plot

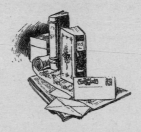

The planned framework of a story you build by selection and arrangement of events creates the structure of a narrative. Therefore, in your novel, the plot itself will be the structural element. The plot takes its shape from what your character says, does, thinks, and from the motives behind the acts.

People read because fiction reveals truths reality obscures. You might have known someone who at least appeared to be just passing through this world, living an unexamined life, but it is not possible to write about a character's existence that has not been scrutinized, contemplated, pondered, probed.

In school we were all given dozens of definitions of "plot." Usually, without the meanings being taken apart, they were deceptively simple, such as, Plot is the system of actions represented in a narrative work. A literal-minded soul could interpret action to mean only physical movement—what you would see if you were deaf and attended a play or a movie. Action in the above sense is meant to include verbal action— conversation—and mental action—the thoughts and feelings of your character. Therefore, plot, the soul of your novel, is the total actions in thought, word, and deed of your characters.

A plot is a planned series of carefully selected, interrelated incidents driven by a struggle between or among opposing forces to a climax and finally to a denouement. The operative word is "planned." If you take your child to the zoo, have a blind date or a dilly of a fight with your boss, you don't have a plot, no matter how hilarious, hideous, or harrowing the episodes might have been. Life lacks the logic of a plot. You can't always figure out what it all means, why things happen and people behave as they do, and events seldom unfold with the neat design of a beginning, a middle, and an end. One of the pleasures of being a writer is imposing order, discovering the essence and purpose in your character's actions. In a well-written story, the question is not *what* happens next, but *why* do things happen as they do; what is the significance of this series of events. Remember the deaths of Forster's king and queen. Plot is the action of your characters selected to emphasize the connection of the happenings or relationships that reveals why these circumstances happen to these particular people. The interest in the story is not the king's death; the drama exists within the queen's broken heart. The intrigue arises from an arrangement of related events establishing a situation with anticipation, suspense, emotion, and satisfaction in a dramatic form. Aristotle added that the incidents must be of adequate importance. He also said the conclusion should be both inevitable and unexpected.

Keep in mind plot is an artificial, rather than a natural, order of events. By concentrating on selected people, emotions, actions, and incidents, you as author simplify life while making it more interesting. Think how tedious it would be to read a story including all thoughts passing through a character's mind on any day, no matter how important, dramatic, or funny.

A warning worth repeating is how beginning writers often tend to overload their plots with dramatic action. The pace moves at the tempo of the chase. The other glib trap is writing like a personal shopper and food taster for the rich and famous. No antibiotic for vicarious living or writing has yet been discovered, but you might reserve an evening with a friend to indulge in a "what-if-we-won-the-lottery fantasy game" and then go back to working on your novel that tells life as it is rather than the way we wish it were.

Sure, many best-selling authors write action-driven plots, called "potboilers," but do you want Aunt Millie to read a review of yours? Satirist Cathleen Schine says she used to think a potboiler was a book bubbling with trashy sex—a beach book—but then she learned it referred to the author's boiling pot 'brimming with meat and potatoes earned through his hack labors, writing—you know—a beach book."

Rather than challenging readers to determine why a character did what he did and what the consequences on his world will be, action stories tend to make the reader eager to find out the story—"And then what happened?"—but not always remember it the next day. A well-thought-out plot rewards the reader with additional insight into the human condition. When you get into your story, you understand your purpose is not to uplift or entertain, but, by coming to understand your character, fearlessly to look for the truth in her despair, her narcissism, her drive, her attraction to whomever. After a reader finishes your novel, he should know your character well enough to predict what happens after the story ends, to know what she would do in a terrorist attack or if she found a lost child.

A memorable plot has a planned purpose. It is about cause and effect. If something happens, there is a result. Hester Prynne commits adultery but refuses to name her lover. The Puritans pin a scarlet letter on her bosom. Hawthorne could have written touching scenes about Pearl and a puppy, or Hester's crippled cousin, Henry, but he chose not to do so because they would have added nothing to his purpose—pursuing the theme of the tragic consequences of concealed guilt.

The most effective plots translate character into action. Billy Budd's fate is determined by his innocence. His simplicity motivates his actions, dialogue, and judgments. The conflict between him and the demonic Claggart rises out of Billy's inability to understand evil's desire to destroy good.

But don't be intimidated by Hawthorne and Melville. You can design an effective, character-driven plot. Let's say your protagonist is motivated by his need to control. How does this need make him behave at work, in a sexual relationship, with his children? What happens when he finds himself in a situation where he has no control—like a traffic jam on the way to an important meeting, when his competent assistant decides to move to California, his rival receives the promotion, his son becomes a ski bum, his wife takes a vacation alone, his mistress falls for a glider instructor?

In the workshop, Marc's character Larry believed in the American dream. Make good grades, don't do anything crazy, pass go and collect your reward on Park Place. He made the

Law Review, was hired by a prestigious firm, put in associate-slave hours, but the economy went soft. The story opens the day he is fired, not because of something he has done wrong, but because there isn't enough business to support young lawyers in his firm or others up and down the avenue. Marc's job is to find out what happens to the best and the brightest when the dream goes sour. After Larry has done everything right, the rules change. The interest in the story is not whom he dated in law school, how tough was his tort final, what he wore to class. His being fired is the cause. How he handles it, why he behaves, feels, and thinks as he does, how his friends and family react, is the effect.

You have a character. You've chosen the period of her life you want to examine. You have ideas about what happened at that time. You've begun to imagine scenes. Now think about unity. Ask yourself if all the episodes you've invented in your tale are relevant to the total meaning or effect of the story. A well-planned plot is like a house of cards. To remove one scene should cause it to fall. Each incident should serve an explainable purpose.

Look at how you have planned to arrange your scenes. Does each event grow logically out of the preceding occurrence? Will the ending—happy, unhappy, or indeterminate—be fairly achieved? By that I mean, will it be inevitable, but not predictable from the beginning? Is this what would have happened under these circumstances to someone like your character? Your mission is to write the way it is, not the way we wish it were.

Danger signs you might have inadvertently absorbed from Hollywood or soap operas: a scoundrel discovers his heart of gold; a coward suddenly finds courage; a handicapped person miraculously walks or regains her vision; you have to invent a deus ex machina such as your character's winning the lottery, finding a rich uncle, being discovered by a talent scout. Wish-fulfillment stories dissolve in the daylight.

When I was a child, every day at lunch Mother and I listened to a radio show that began with the question, "Can this girl from a small mining town in the West find happiness as the wife of a wealthy and titled Englishman?" Growing up convinced I could, I still feel gypped that my wealthy and titled Englishman never came along. Don't gyp your readers.

- ✍ In a paragraph, summarize what your story is about, such as: in Abilene, rebel Charlie Bob Blake, twenty, joins the rodeo to prove his manhood to his father, the champ. On the circuit, he makes friends with Joey Bill and falls in love with Lucy-Anne. Three years later, in Cheyenne, he competes with his father for the championship. He wins/loses/lets his father win. As a result _____.

- ✍ Summarize, not the story, but what it means, such as: maturity doesn't necessarily involve winning; winning can feel like losing; passing the torch is the natural order of things, or _____.

- ✍ As you begin each chapter, using words like "to show," "to establish," "to reveal," "to move," "to develop," list the purpose you intend to accomplish. For example: in the flashback to a scene in Charlie Bob's childhood, told from his father's point of view, I want to show that the boy mistakenly interprets his father's reserved nature for rejection. I intend to reveal that the older man thinks it is his responsibility as a father to raise a boy to be tough so he can't be pushed around. I want to create dramatic irony so the reader understands the problematic situation and its effect, as neither the boy nor his father does.

- ✍ How do you set up the scene to achieve your aim? Where is the hub of the incident? What do you need to accentuate—your character's mood, his thoughts, the conversation he has with _____, the setting _____ _____?

- ✍ When you complete a chapter, ask yourself what the consequences will be. Will the effect be immediate, or will other things have to happen before you show the outcome?

CHAPTER 11

Biting the Bullet: Writing Your Novel

THE LAST LINE

Salute! So you wanted to write a novel and now you're going to do it! You've honored your schedule, found your character, understood his motivation, uncovered his story, made the agonizing decisions about conflict, time, place, point of view. You've accomplished the most difficult part.

BEGIN. Write the last line.

The last line is the narrator's or your character's farewell to the reader. After you've decided how to say good-bye, put it in your notebook. For the next year or so, your character will climb mountains, slide back, fall down, get up, try again. Where will he be when the trip is over? In good literature, the end is only the beginning, unless your character dies, which is often a beginning writer's cop-out. But unless it is absolutely inevitable, I'd bet you couldn't bear to part with your character you know as well as your brother. But something must have happened to this person who has walked through three or four hundred pages of thoughts and events. Perhaps he has caught a glimpse of the light, or maybe he is going in the opposite direction. For example, on an ironic but hopeful note, Frankie says, "At least the commercial planes have higher ceilings."

You might change the last line, have your swan sing a different song, but until you discover something about your character and his story that you don't know when you begin, having a finale in mind keeps you in step. Writing an ending that is inescapable but not foreseen is easier when you work backward.

Stories never end. The sun will come up the morning following the last page. Making that decision in the beginning about what portion of his life to probe will tell you when to quit. The last line is like reaching the sign that says: "Congratulations! You have reached the top of the mountain."

E X E R C I S E S

∞   My last line implies that my character has:

> *come to grips*
> *given up hope*
> *beaten the bastard*
> *learned his lesson*
> *missed the point*
> *found peace*
> *turned in another direction*
> *accomplished his mission*
> *realized it wasn't important*
> *destroyed his chances*
> *set a new goal*
> *given her up*
> *changed his priorities*
> *saved someone else*
> *beaten the system*
> *grown up*
> *come to understand*
> *forgiven them*

∞   I want the tone of my last line to be hopeful, dour, funny, ironic, wise, judgmental, serious, or _____ _____.

∞   The person who gets the last line is the narrator, my character, another character commenting about my protagonist, a newspaper reporter, a TV anchorman, a judge, the preacher, or _____.

     ☞   My story is fated to end as it does because my character is _____, human nature is _____ _____, or society is _____ _____.

     ☞   The reader might think or hope _____ would happen, which would cause the story to end differently. This could not happen because _____ _____.

THE FIRST LINE

If you have a fascinating story and character, buckle up. It's going to be a thrilling, hairy ride. If you're lucky, the character dictates as you roll along, you write it down, but you are the driver. Each writing period begins with your asking him, "Okay, then what happened? Was X involved? How did you feel about that? Why did you do it? But why didn't you tell X? Are you trying to hide something from me?"

Don't let the first line become a roadblock. Since 1851, writers have dreamed of finding an opener to knock "Call me Ishmael" out of first place. But in *The Plague*, Camus's writer, who spent twenty years reworking the same first line, made the theory of the absurd perfectly clear. Granted, you want a gripper to lure the reader (but first an editor or an agent) into your story. You want to beguile, entice, seduce, mesmerize, bewitch, tickle, bait. But what you don't want to do is face an intimidating blank sheet of paper until you're the one who is spellbound.

Perhaps you will change it thirteen times, but start to speak before you lose your nerve. You have a story to tell. With the last line stashed in your notebook, you know where you're going. Remember Kerr's gossipy mother. Pretend you are saying to your best friend, "Wait till you hear this."

Perhaps your story is about adult sibling rivalry. "Sam's life lost its luster when he was three." Or, "Sam's wife had disliked his sister even before she realized Lydia had broken up their marriage without ever paying a visit or picking up the phone." Or, "Three hours after the others had gone, Sam sat in his office writing another letter to his sister he knew when he started he would never send."

You have three choices for your opening: *narration,* as in the examples above, in which a narrator is telling the reader there is a problem to resolve, a question to answer. The story could have opened with a *description* of the setting or the main character. Some stories open with *scenes* that offer readers an immediate, direct encounter with the characters. They hear them talk, see them in action, as we do when we watch a movie. A dramatic beginning can grasp readers' attention, but the drawback is their not having been prepared to catch the nuances in the conversation, see the significance of the details in the episode. The disadvantage is slight, however. Readers don't expect everything to be perfectly clear at first and will usually stick with you until you have explained the relevance.

Think of novels you have loved from the beginning. Perhaps you were hooked by a tongue-in-cheek narrative style, an unusual point of view captured your attention, the mood or the atmosphere carried you right out of your reading chair into the character's world, or you were immediately concerned about or emotionally involved with this person. Some writers can describe a place with such sparkling detail, such clear images, that it is like taking a mini-vacation.

Not all stories plunge right into the heart of the matter, but don't wait too long. An editor deciding to publish a story is like you browsing in a bookstore. How much do you read before you have decided if you want to buy the novel? Be a bold writer. Jump in. Don't be like the toastmaster who goes rambling on and on before he gets to his subject. You won't have an audience when you are finally ready to start your tale.

Showing your stuff immediately is especially important if there is a unique angle to your novel, such as if it is told from the point of view of someone who is demonic, naive, bitter, ignorant, defensive, hurt, a victim, a joker. Or if the story is set in the future, in a native village, on a warship, show what is peculiar, original, atypical, or curious, preferably in the first line.

E X E R C I S E S

⤷ The unique aspect of my story is:

> the point of view
> the time and place
> the humor
> the complexity of my protagonist
> what happens to her
> why it happens to her
> her relationship with _____
> the power of her antagonist
> her conflict with _____
> her past
> her attitude
> her lack of _____
> her success
> her failure

⤷ The best way for me to reveal what is distinctive about my story is to open with:

> a description of _____
> the narrator explaining _____
> a scene showing my character _____
> alone or with _____
> conversation between _____

KEEPING YOUR NOVEL MOVING

You have a first and last line. Giant steps! Now all you have to do is write one page per day for the next year. If you have a fascinating character with a good story, you will feel cheated when you aren't able to make time to write. To keep the momentum going, you will make the rules.

Don't forget helpful hints other writers have offered:

⤷ Find a comfortable, permanent, preferably private, place to work that you don't have to make tidy after each working session.

◌ Buy that answering machine. Connect it near your typewriter. Earlier I said you will know you are a writer when HE calls or SHE calls and you keep typing. However, Maria says she feels less guilt and anxiety if she returns all her calls before she starts to work.

◌ Wear what is comfortable, or if you are superstitious, what brings you good luck, such as your high school track jersey or Bloomie's t-shirt. I still can't write with my shoes on, but footware is your decision.

◌ Put yourself in the right frame of mind. Pat and Chip, the dog-lovers in the workshop, walk their pets first. Guilt, they say does not spark creativity. Before she begins, Heather has a cleansing ritual that to less imaginative types might look only like a shower.

◌ Keep your story in mind, no matter where you are or what you are doing. Most important: WRITE REGULARLY. Slipping off your schedule results in a loss of momentum, memory, and motivation.

◌ Follow Hemingway's advice. Stop for the day when you still have something to say, knowing where you are going to begin next time. You will be thinking about it and probably enrich the scene while you're doing something else, such as singing in the choir or shining your shoes. Most important: keep that notebook handy for a splendid idea.

◌ Remember the perverse imp whose name is Procrastination, the one who will tempt you to reread your entire manuscript before you write a word. Fool him. Reread only a portion and don't listen to him when he suggests you order a pizza, do the crossword puzzle, or dash out to buy Aunt Tilly a birthday card.

◌ If your muse takes a holiday or becomes sullen, try some of the warm-up exercises listed in the back of the book.

BECOMING YOUR OWN EDITOR AND CRITIC

"Education is wasted on the young" plays like a refrain in your mind when finally you would pay for information an unappreciated teacher tried assiduously to give you for free.

How did you know you were going to write a novel when Miss Brooks strained to explain verb tense agreement, the passive voice? Remember how everybody giggled, thinking she had a lisp when she said "pluperfect," and guffawed when Billy Barnes said the subjunctive mood was what Miss Brooks was in when she had her period?

Don't quit writing. It happens to all of us. Packed away in the attic you probably have a grammar handbook from seventh grade or Rhetoric 101. Unpack it and blow off the dust. If you can't remember if the quotation mark goes inside or outside the question mark, looking it up will be easier than tracking down your oldest sister or roommate from freshman year, both of whom seemed to have been born with all those rules branded on their brains. This time you'll get it. Learning is easier when you have a need to know.

Lucky you, if Miss Brooks got your attention. You won't have to bother with the following.

Punctuating Dialogue and Thoughts

Where to put a comma is not as important as where to put your character, but clean it up. Just as you wouldn't buy a spotted Brooks Brothers suit, an editor is less apt to buy a manuscript dappled with errors. Following are a few examples of how conversation and thoughts look on a page. If remembering rules of grammar is your specialty, skip to the next section.

"Myra's husband wouldn't think of going to the club without a tie. He always looks like a prince," she said, slamming the cabinet door with a shove from her plump derriere. "Maybe that's why he's a vice president."

"What are you implying?"

"Forget it! Just forget it. Do I care? Even when the children are ashamed of their sloppy father," she said, "there is nothing I can do. It's not my problem, is it?"

I can barely remember when those swaying hips of hers stunned me, he thought as he watched his wife strut out of the room swinging her bouncy behind more than necessary.

Check Your Verbs

Remember to avoid passive verbs—"The girl was kissed by John"—as you would killer bees, unless you're using them in conversation to show a character is ducking being held responsible for an action.

Be certain you've picked the most powerful and most explicit verbs. Would your character walk, stride, stroll, saunter, skip, amble, down the street?

Euphemistic verbs smell of prudery unless you are trying to portray a fussbudget. Then they are character developers. Fuddy-duddies step in deep doo-doo.

Clear Away the Jumble

Americans hold rummage sales, but when British attics become so cluttered people can't tell what is what, they remove the jumble. Call it what you will, but you can bet on having collected some litter in your manuscript.

Begin with weasel words. You know their type. You have some in your office. They take up space, try to look important, but don't do a lick of work. "That" is the prize weasel. "That," more than any other freeloader, with the exception of "you know" or "you know what I mean" in teenager's talk, worms its way into sentences where it isn't needed. "I thought that I would take a walk." It is impossible to think "that." "He said that I could go." "That" is not what he said at all. Also, look closely at "which." Speaking of which, we usually do not need. As to "as to," use "about" if you must, but usually neither is necessary. "As to our relationship, I'm dumping you" takes too long to reach the jugular.

Concise, Precise, Clear, Short

Of course you want to be clever, original, impressive, but essayist John Dryden got it right in the seventeenth century when he said, "The chief aim of the writer is to be understood."

"Precise" and "concise" always correlate with "clear" and often with "short." Beginning fiction writers with backgrounds in the professions—law, education, medicine, religion—and especially in business and government have to break bad habits to write clearly. We call the long-winded "language of" taught in those schools businessese, medicalese, etc. Your daily mail brings bloated messages from the IRS, the schools, your boss. They read like this: "It would appear that with future planning during one or more of these preliminary steps, the execution of our project can be completed in our projected period of time."

The rules in "ese" seem to be: never use one simple word like "time" when you can smother it in phrases like "projected period of time"; never explain precisely what action is being taken by whom, so no one can ever be blamed; never use clear language people understand, or they won't think you are smarter than they are; use redundancies like "future planning" (or my favorite—"brief moment") because your reader is not intelligent enough to understand unless you tell him twice.

In John's academic satire, he created a professor who gave a three-page lecture on deconstructionism. Using language from the field, but understood only in the land of "ese," he was able to put together 750 real words in their correct syntax, so that not one person in the group, even Alice with three degrees in the classics, could make sense of a single sentence.

People addicted to "ese" are usually preposition junkies too. They "listen up," "continue on," "meet with," "tear up," when they could "listen," "continue," "meet," or "destroy."

Fiction writers imitate language to make their characters look and sound like real people who are pompous, cowardly, intimidated, pretentious, ridiculous, ignorant, bigoted, narrow-minded, self-conscious, domineering, but they edit their narration to make it as lucid as possible.

Use the following as guidelines to clear away your jumble. When you raise your clutter awareness, your antenna will find others to add.

AVOID	SUGGESTED SUBSTITUTE
ask the question	ask
assemble together	assemble
along the lines of	like
at the present time	now
currently	now
presently	now
has possession of	has
in the case of	if
in connection with	of, in, on
in a satisfactory manner	satisfactorily

Avoid	Suggested Substitute
each and every	each, or every
consensus of opinion	consensus
due to the fact that	because
the reason is because	because
for the purpose of	for
implement	do
referred to as	called
nethergarment	britches
unmentionables	underwear
boobies	breasts
interface	unite, talk
input	place, idea

Misplaced Modifiers

You have added details to clarify the image your reader has of your character, her action, a setting, an idea. Check to see if the modifying word or phrase is as close as possible to the word it is meant to enhance. "Jane shampooed the poodle John had given her with loving strokes" confuses because the reader is not sure if Jane or John used the loving strokes. If you write, "My broker almost lost my entire investment," when you intended to say, "My broker lost almost my entire investment," you have changed the meaning. "Mary only mourned the closing of her company" forces the reader to decide if Mary were the only employee who cared, or if the closing of her office was the only thing she ever mourned.

Clichés, Purple Prose, and Mixed, Farfetched, Packed Metaphors

Fresh figurative language and descriptive details illuminate your story. A stale cliché dulls it. Putting trite expressions like "the early bird gets the worm" in a tedious or boring character's mouth to show he has a lazy mind might work, but if you as narrator use banal or hackneyed ideas, guess whose laziness will be showing? Unthinking use of ready-made phrases skate over the meaning, as politicians often do by labeling a suggestion a "knee-jerk liberal idea" or a bill a "tax and spend" plan. Placing a cliché in quotation marks "won't fly" either. It proves you know better, but aren't willing to make the effort to find a novel way to express the idea or show the image.

Purple prose goes beyond being flowery or syrupy. It is the kind of language you would be embarrassed to use in conversation. I just know you would never say, "In the bright, fiery heat of my wild moment of passion with Jason, I finally realized what it meant to be a woman, loved, cherished, and adored." Not only does overblown language draw upon every known synonym for heat and fire, but it blubbers sentimentality about the loss of anything and lovers who've done someone you couldn't bear to have lunch with wrong.

Mary Lee Settle's *Charley Bland* became one of my favorite novels when I read the opening line. The metaphor "all wild roads led to Charley Bland" took me prisoner. I had been trying to write that line all my life . . . or loving the man who inspired it. The book is too good to miss, but you don't really have to read the rest of the story. You know it. Probably lived it, unless you're one of those fortunate souls who never fell for the wrong person. Settle didn't use her image to embellish. It expressed a dreadful truth and is a metaphor for the entire story. It's a short book. I read every chapter twice to make it last longer.

You are developing your style based on the way you think and view the world. Be it spare like Raymond Carver's or poetic like William Faulkner's, it can tell a moving story. As long as you don't expect the audience to read your mind, a lean style might be easier to control, but if you use common sense, a lyrical view of your character's cosmos can be delightful.

Most important, don't overload. Laying image upon image, detail upon detail, is like looking through a kaleidoscope, where the picture changes too quickly to remember. What happens when you read, "The bad boy, the one with the dirty face and raccoon eyes, could run like an antelope and sneer like a Holy Roller"? Comparing him with animals as unlike as a raccoon and an antelope, neither of which is known to be dirty or bad, is confusing enough, but to mix in the religious reference is so farfetched it's silly.

Judging the Effectiveness of a Sex Scene

Writers joke, usually nervously, about their OSS (obligatory sex scene). "Obligatory" is the operative word. If your story logically builds to a point where the reader needs to know if they did it, you are obliged to tell it or show it. However, if you've been reading a lot of recently published fiction and those writers all have a sex scene, so you suppose you'd better have one too, my suggestion is forget it. "All the other kids are doing it" was a better argument when you were thirteen.

Approaches to writing about sex reflect as much as anything about the values of an age. In the University of Chicago Great Books Discussion Group I direct for New York alumni, we recently read Thomas Mann's *Magic Mountain* and spent a long time simply trying to determine if Hans Castorp "had carnal knowledge" of Claudia Chauchat. Mann would have turned over in his grave if we had tried to determine if he "fucked" her. But at that time, German writers were not alone in closing the bedroom door. We also read Dreiser's *Sister Carrie*, who lived "out of wedlock" with Charles Droulet and George Hurstwood. The novel created such a stir in America, it was withheld from publication for twelve years, but we could find only one bedroom scene, and it was set when Carrie entered the room after Hurstwood had fallen asleep.

The best advice about writing sex scenes I've been able to find comes from Tennessee Williams, who said if you don't want to do whatever they're doing, delete it or start over. Williams also said he couldn't write unless he desired at least one of the characters. In *A Streetcar Named Desire* when you realize Blanche's viewpoint is his, not only do the scenes between her and the handsome, brutish Stanley become more poignant, but the anguish of the playwright's life makes sense.

This is a subjective view, but I've wanted to do what they're doing less since licking replaced kissing. Try as I may, the image of Fang, a friend's chummy but ill-mannered German shepherd, comes to mind when a character is being licked from her earlobe to her little toe. A kiss on the palm of a hand still works for me.

When I asked for group feedback after a woman in the workshop read a sex scene as graphic as anything D. H. Lawrence or Henry Miller ever wrote, Steven, a handsome bachelor, said, "I want your character's phone number." "Voila!" the ecstatic writer said. "Lust was what I was after!"

The language for love or lust is different, and lust is easier. The language is spicier. If what your character feels is lust, decide how to shade his emotion. Would his feeling be best described as an appetite, eroticism, salaciousness, lewdness, lechery, sensuality, racy, ribald, risqué, vulgar, indecent, earthy, obscene, pornographic? I had to look up "concupiscence," a show-off word meaning a strong sexual desire that probably wouldn't make many readers' hearts pound. Love, also, is measured by degrees, but the language temperature is lower, like in adoration, passion, infatuation, devotion, worship.

After you've determined if your character's blood pressure is high or low, you have to decide if you can create graphic details to capture the essence of your episode that have not been overused to the point of making a highly charged scene boring or unreal. If all else fails, you can always have your character come out of the bedroom with a smile on his face or whistling a chipper tune.

Verb Tense Agreement

You chose the tense when you made the decision to tell your story, OSS and all, as if it were unfolding at this moment (present tense), or as if it took place yesterday, a year ago, or in the seventeenth century (past tense). With the exception of flashbacks, where you use the past perfect tense (had seen), stick to your choice.

It is a good idea to edit as often as at the bottom of each page for careless switches like "When the baby died, Mary freezes instead of cries."

Don't ask me why "lie," "lay," "sit," "set," such little words, can intimidate the bravest of writers. If they don't scare you, skip ahead. The easiest way to straighten them out is to remember you have to have something (an object) to lay or set. "She lay the baby in the crib." "He set my gift on the desk." "Lie" and "sit" do not have objects. I lie alone. He sits. The present tense is easier because the form changes for the past. "Yesterday she lay in bed until noon." Having the forms in front of you could help:

Present	Past	Past Participle
lie (recline)	lay	(I have) lain
lay (deposit)	laid	laid
lie (falsify)	lied	lied
sit	sat	sat
set	set	set

The agreement rule changes when you express a condition contrary to fact: "If he were here"; a doubt or uncertainty: "If this disease be contagious"; a wish: "Would that he were here"; necessity: "It is urgent he leave immediately"; or a parliamentary motion: "I move that he go alone."

This exception, known as the subjunctive mood, does what it promises, changes the mood or tone of your writing. If your character becomes dreamy or forlorn, she will slip into the subjunctive mood, saying things like, "If I were anchor on the evening news," "If only I were his wife," but it can also show assertiveness: "I suggest she move now."

Number Agreement

Editing immediately for subject and verb agreement is another good habit, and will save time when you have a first draft. If you say, "The children and the dog gets on my nerves," it is probably an oversight. If you fudge because you're not certain "each" and "everyone" are singular nouns, keep your seventh-grade grammar book handy. "Each of the pages is filled with helpful editing information."

Trying to be politically correct yet avoid the awkwardness of "he/she" (singular) often causes writers to substitute "their" (plural) with a singular verb. Sorry; even if Gloria Steinem were your editor, she might admire your sentiment but wouldn't let you get away with breaking the agreement rule.

Nominative, Objective, Possessive Case

Between you and me, the grammatical errors that can give me a toothache most often come from people who are trying the hardest. I once had a rags-to-riches boss whose lack of a formal education tormented him. He overcompensated with alacrity, especially when he said "between you and *I*," with a strong emphasis on the incorrect "I." Soap opera actors are stars at object-of-preposition errors such as, "Will you go with Brandy and *I*?" Perhaps the scriptwriters think "I" sounds more proper than the correct "with Brandy and me"? Who knows.

The rules seem simple enough. Subjects of verbs require the nominative case—I, you, he, we, you, they. Objects of verbs and prepositions take the objective case—me, you, him, her, it, us, them. The possessive case—my, mine, your, yours, his, her, hers, its, our, ours, your, yours, their, theirs—indicates ownership.

The exceptions and complicated structures are what drive you nuts. It helps if you have studied Latin. Here are a few exceptions, but keep your handbook handy.

It is *I*. (Linking verbs have subjective complements, not objects; therefore, use the nominative case.)

His attending was an unexpected pleasure. (Gerunds, the "ing" forms of verbs used as nouns, take the possessive case.)

The actor and the model whom he loved had a spat. ("Whom" is the object of "loved.")

Whom do you think him to be? (Subjects, objects, and subjective complements of infinitives—"to be" form of verbs—require the objective case.

Shift in Viewpoint

You knew, when you chose your point of view, staying put would not always be easy. Don't be tempted "just this once," "only in this one scene," to switch. The flag you wave says "Amateur at work here." But don't be discouraged; you can find a way around your problem.

Julie had created a scene in a cab, told from Dan's point of view immediately after the death of his father. But she slipped into the driver's thoughts to comment on Dan's strange behavior and disheveled appearance. Dan couldn't say he looked awful and was acting funny, but she could restructure the scene so the driver, looking in the rearview mirror, could put his thoughts into words and say to Dan, "Man, you're about to ruin my upholstery with all your flopping around. You okay? It's none of my business, but you don't look so good either. . . ."

When you've inadvertently shifted from the perspective you're using, ask yourself what information the reader needs to know that you can't offer from your narrator's view. What are other options? Could you put it in a letter, newspaper article, diary; could the information be overheard; could another character tell it?

Repetition

Check for words and phrases that keep popping up over and over. Unless repeating a word for clarity is necessary, never use it more than once in the same paragraph, and not on the same page if an appropriate synonym exists. If your character is dealing with a memory, she can say she "remembers," "recalls," "recollects." The "remembrance" can be "evoked," "roused," "summoned," "elicited."

Often a word will creep out of our subconscious and attach itself everywhere. Recently I wrote, "Sunday was a fine day," which was perfectly okay, but when I scanned the page, I found a "fine boy," a "fine time," and a "fine meal," which wasn't so fine.

"Time" permeates many manuscripts. "Get" and "made" are the most overused verbs after forms of "to be." "At first" or "in the beginning" works "fine" the first time.

Repeating the same sentence structure and approximate length wrecks the rhythm. "John loves Mary," "Mary prefers Peter," "Peter cares for Tom," thud when they should flow. You could combine them: "John is in love with Mary, but she prefers Peter, which complicates the situation even more since he cares for Tom." One of many other variations: "Although John loves Mary, she prefers Peter. Since Peter cares for Tom, affairs are in a muddle."

Reading your work aloud often helps to spot repetitions and discord. Overusing your character's name rather than a pronoun or more "he saids" than necessary for clarity can also become boring. You'll hear it.

Political Correctness Binging

Of course you don't want to offend or hurt anyone, but you do want to create reality and avoid an obvious self-conscious style.

If all your powerful people are female, Irish characters drink milk, the Italians say mass every day, the gays are all in monogamous relationships, the good guys are black or Hispanic, the bad guys are white—pull up on the reins. The Mafia does still exist. And the civil rights movement did not purify every African American soul.

In the nineties, Mary Gordon was not arrested by the political correctness police, and she received a *New York Times Book Review* front-page review for *The Rest of Life,* about three women in "helping professions," each focused on some man with whom she is involved in an "obsessive, unequal sexual relationship."

Don't make your story read as if you are trying too hard.

What Is Driving Your Plot?

In memorable stories, the protagonist's character is responsible for what happens. An obsessive nature can create a lot of chaos. If Ahab hadn't been obsessed, Moby Dick would have died of natural causes without all those scars, and none of us would have had to read those boring chapters about whaling. If Gatsby hadn't been obsessed with Daisy, no one would give a hoot how many monogrammed shirts he owned.

Earlier, we discussed avoiding the beginning-writer pitfall of creating nightmares, tornadoes, train wrecks, monsters, mysterious strangers, murders, when you are afraid you are boring the reader. Boiling a lobster can be a rollicking adventure when you know how your character feels about murder or cooking or creatures—even awkward, ugly ones with menacing claws, which turn red with anger when you . . . you know . . . boil them alive.

If you find you are forced to think of a dramatic event to keep the story going, you might not have come to understand your protagonist well enough to imagine what would motivate him. You might know your character finds it difficult to express his feelings, especially to people he loves, but you might not have delved into what past experience or relationship was the genesis of this behavior. Perhaps he opened his heart to someone who took advantage of him or made him feel foolish. Perhaps the person he most admired in his youth was detached, taciturn, reserved, inhibited. Perhaps he was raised by a narcissistic parent.

After you have deduced a possible reason for his behavior,

continue to peel away. Many people survive unrequited love
without permanent scars. Was the reason for your character's being damaged the rare force or attraction of the person
he adored, or his lack of self-confidence to rebuild his ego?
Let's say it was the power or charisma of the person he cherished. Did the object of his affection actually possess the
charm and magnetism, or did he give these qualities to the
individual, manufacturing the uniqueness in his imagination
as Gatsby did for Daisy?

When you have answers, the next step is to invent ways to
show the reader your discoveries. You could do flashbacks
from your character's viewpoint or weave snatches of his
memories into many scenes. Another person from his past
could talk to him about the experience. A scene showing conflicting portraits presented by your character and the other
individual could be dramatic.

In the workshop, writers working on mysteries will often
say, "But action is supposed to drive the plot in my genre."
Not necessarily so. The most successful and enduring mystery series, like those of Sherlock Holmes and Nero Wolfe, are
character-driven.

You warm up before you play basketball or run. Ideas can
stiffen as well as your muscles, especially when not put to
work regularly. Starting your writing day with exercises is not
goofing off, even if you have reached page 225.

Read that last line sitting boldly in your notebook like a
wreath of roses at the finish line. Then have a chat with your
character. Let him do most of the talking. Here is how it
might sound:

> This is your character speaking. If we are ever going to reach
> the place where I can finally pick up the phone to make that
> call in the last line, we have to work through some stuff, or
> nobody in hell is going to believe I have the guts to do it. The
> courage is down there, but it's still covered with anger, guilt,
> and to be honest, I'm still scared that . . .

You know where you are going and what is going to happen, but the reader should not. However, when she reads
that line, even if it is not the way she had been hoping the
story would end, she had to say it's okay. Such an ending
was inescapable for this person.

Don't worry about being a plodder or a sprinter. Writing a

novel is a marathon. Your time isn't important; reaching the finish line is. A page a day is a good pace, but if you can't do that, keep on chugging.

SO YOU HAVE A *FIRST* DRAFT

Good golly, Miss Molly, you have finally written in that last line! Voila! You have finished a first draft.

You did it! Give yourself a reward. Brag, boast, pat yourself on the back, tap-dance—on the table if you feel like it. Go to the carnival, have a feast, walk barefoot in the dewy grass. Hold a jubilee, and a jamboree. Multitudes would like to, myriads say they are going to . . . sometime, but you wrote a novel from that tough first line to a conclusion. You deserve your revelry.

After the deserved celebration:

Read your story from cover to cover, ALOUD, in one sitting if possible. Note loose ends, like a character introduced who was supposed to reappear but didn't, a man who was called Corky on page 10 and Carl on page 125, an important letter someone mailed but no one ever received. Be alert for black holes—the pacing slows to a crawl, the narrator telling rather than the character showing how he felt or why he acted, you forgetting to tell the reader something she needs to know. One scene in the moonlight could have been written by a romance writer.

Prepare to be surprised. You learn to write by writing. You will have improved your style to the extent of disclaiming some earlier passages. After Pat finished her first draft, she said, "The first five chapters are embarrassing." *Fix them* is the answer to that dilemma. By the time you've completed the first version, you will understand techniques like transitions, flashbacks, structuring, in a way only trying and retrying can teach. Your character? The things you've learned about him, even his mother doesn't know. You will apply the new insights to your revision.

Know thyself is the next stage. Before you begin again, I suggest you take a vacation. However, if you are an obsessive-compulsive type, you'll simply take the manuscript with you. It will be cheaper and more comfortable to work at home. Then there are workaholics. I still remember, years ago, Joyce Carol Oates's stunning dinner-party guests by saying the worst kind of torture she could imagine would be vacationing on the most beautiful beach in the world. You can tell from her output that woman LOVES to work.

If you do snatch a holiday, here's what I propose. Before packing, read the story, make notes, and then put the manuscript in a drawer. Okay, if you're manic, rent a lockbox. I have a friend who keeps her manuscript in the refrigerator overnight, in case the house burns down.

Having practiced the method-acting technique of writing for such a long time, you realize there is absolutely no way you can get out of town without your character, but that's good. Thinking through the story and plot, problems you have to mend, can go on while you are snorkeling, skiing, skating, or sailing. You'll probably come back with ideas as fresh as the mountain or sea air you breathed.

Here I feel like the stockbroker who tells you when to buy, but never when to sell. I can tell you when and why to begin revisions. The gods who look after writers will have to tell you when to stop. I no longer remember the novelist's name, but I recall his saying your story is never finished. Finally you simply abandon it. But don't tell yourself a good editor will add the spit and polish.

Maxwell Perkins died years ago. The position for the nurturing editor who will correct your spelling, cut the deadwood, and pay your bills will not be filled. Publishing stopped being a gentleman's or a gentleperson's business when the first conglomerate took its first bite and liked the taste so much it devoured almost the entire industry. If you don't work on a computer, type your story, or hire a typist to prepare a religiously corrected copy in proper manuscript style. The way it looks on the page is important. This poor speller genuflects daily to whoever invented spellcheck. It's best not to turn in a manuscript with grammatical errors, misspellings, hand corrections. Only published writers whose first printing is 100,000 copies can do that.

There is another caveat, however. No editor is going to reject a wonderful book because the author just can't get it into his head there's no apostrophe in "its" unless it's a contraction for "it is." Be professional, but don't get so paralyzed with fear you never submit your manuscript.

FINDING AN AGENT, GETTING PUBLISHED

Finding an agent can be as difficult and as frustrating as finding a mate. It is a marriage of sorts, but it's worth the effort and it's practical. Having someone to represent you im-measurably improves your chances of being published.

Here is how it works. An established agent has contacts. Either she can be respected because she doesn't try to push schlock, or she can have power because she represents authors whom houses would like to publish. If you get an interview with an agent, the first question is "Whom do you represent?"

When an agent submits your manuscript, it will be read . . . and more "timely," you will be told. Don't rely on your dictionary's definition of "timely." In publishing language, it doesn't mean promptly. A reply in three months is timely. Most houses still follow the old, gentleman's agreement that even unsolicited manuscripts will be read. However, in that case, "time" could be a year. Having become sensitive to language, you will note the significance of "slush pile," the insider's term for unsolicited manuscripts. The submissions that come "over the transom" (sent by the author, without an agent) are given to editorial assistants or readers. A friend who is a reader calls herself "a hired gun." There could be exceptions, especially in smaller houses, but this is generally the procedure. She reads "not very much" of what she doesn't like, but when a voice is good, a character appealing, a style unique, she reads it all. If the story holds up, she recommends a second reading in-house, usually by an assistant. If he likes it too, the editor receives it.

Also, an agent should know editors' tastes and be able to make the best match for your manuscript. Some editors prefer long books, perhaps sagas. Others have a propensity for literary stories, or historic novels, or mysteries. If you have written a gay story, your chances are better with an editor who has published others.

When it comes to negotiating a contract, agents will also have more clout and history to rely on. Although royalties and rights splits are pretty standard for first-time authors, agents will know how far to push for a larger advance, when it's prudent to save the tough negotiations for the royalties or rights (movies, TV, serials, audio, foreign sales, etc). Unless you have the hottest property of the season, editors will find it easier to refuse your demands than those of a powerful agent's who might send his next discovery to another house.

Convincing you that you need an agent is easier than telling you how to find one. If your manuscript has obvious commercial potential, something unique the world has been waiting for, or is just so damned good, finding an agent won't be so hard. But usually it takes persistence, patience, and contacts, contacts, contacts.

In the workshop, Colleen, who writes children's stories about middle-class black kids, had no trouble finding an agent. Publishers are eager for such stories, and she also writes well. John sent three chapters of his academic satire to four agents and got a bite. I'm not alone in thinking his work is exceptional.

I can promise you writing your story will be more fun than selling it, but leaving you with the impression you absolutely must have an agent would be wrong. Finding an agent can be almost as difficult as finding a publisher, and even then you don't have a contract, so if you don't find one, don't give up. Try your luck by submitting directly to publishing houses. Here are some rules to follow:

- ☞ Do research. Look in bookstores to see who publishes books similar to yours, an indication of an editorial sensibility that might be responsive to your book.

- ☞ Call a publisher before submitting your manuscript to learn if that house accepts unsolicited manuscripts without a query or if it accepts multiple submissions. Don't waste the time and postage with a blind submission.

- ☞ Keep your cover letter short and to the point. Editors tell me cute doesn't get attention, it just looks unprofessional.

- ☞ Use your contacts. Talk to every writer you know. Ask for suggestions and information. A phone call works best, but "so-and-so suggested I . . ." can also be effective in a letter. Go to readings and seminars, form a writing group, join professional organizations. Meet as many people as you can to learn about the business.

If you turn up no leads, look at *Writer's Market*. This helpful guide contains advice on selling your book as well as lists of publishers and agents with their addresses and phone numbers.

GOOD LUCK!

Extra Exercises

- Your character once heard her father say, "Oh, sure, I have a nice daughter, but it's not the same, you know what I mean?" She knew what he meant, and she has never forgotten.

- Your character goes into a church to light a candle. He lights them all. Explain why he is there, why he changes his mind, and how he feels about his decision.

- It had been good, but it was over. Other doors had been slammed decisively, others left ajar, but this one your character closed regretfully and softly.

- Your character has a killer pattern of behavior in choosing companions, making decisions, or _____ _____. Over and over she _____ _____.

- Your character ties his dog to a gum machine that he pulls over and breaks. Kids, lots of kids, appear. Describe the scene. Concentrate on details.

- "My definition of a good sport is _____ _____," your character says.

- Write about a haircut.

- "It's the eyeglasses that are wrong," your character says. "They make him look _____."

- ❧ Your character sits next to someone whose headphones are leaking a dreadful sound. Describe the scene and the sound.

- ❧ Your character makes sacrifices for _____ _____, not because she loves her/him, but because it makes her feel saintly.

- ❧ "Trouble never has any problem finding me," your character says when _____.

- ❧ Write an interior monologue in which your character decides she can't trust anyone except herself.

- ❧ If everything in your story is predictable, it will be boring. Give a "not what you expect" twist to one of the following:

a death	*a race*	*a letter*
a kiss	*a homecoming*	*a baby*
a vacation	*a raise*	

- ❧ Appealing to all the senses, write about oysters on the half shell.

- ❧ A boa constrictor kills by taking up the slack when his victim breathes in. Use his method as a symbol in your story.

- ❧ Describe an action scene. Take your character to the races, sailing in a storm, rollerblading; he fights or observes one. Try to make the reader feel as if she is there, seeing, hearing, feeling, the experience.

- ❧ Writing is putting words to music. Make something jig—an egg boiling, a boat, a street entertainer . . . Concentrate on the rhythm.

- ❧ Putting tap water in his Evian bottle was not the only thing he did to keep up appearances.

- ❧ They were too horribly entertaining and too entertainingly horrible, but no matter how treacherously venomous they were, your character came back for more.

- ❧ Her mother had always described him as a decent, dull dog, but your character knew he could bite.

- ❧ Your character solves his problem by creative chicanery.

ᵒ❥ Your character meets a child who is as skinny as a stray cat and as resourceful.

ᵒ❥ "For me, the toughest audience in the world is _____ _____," your character says.

ᵒ❥ _____ hadn't been a significant player in her life for a long time, yet it was most often his criteria she used to evaluate.

ᵒ❥ "I don't believe in toys for grown-ups," your character says.

ᵒ❥ "This is more proof that you have a diamond-hard ego," someone says to your character.

ᵒ❥ Charm and dramatic "poor me" stories had worked for years. Finally, maybe it was accumulative—their disbelief, her guilt, or maybe age—but they began not to work so well.

ᵒ❥ The wedding was scheduled for four. At two, without a backward glance, he boarded a plane for Singapore.

ᵒ❥ The chance to _____ gave your character the opportunity to be the Peter Pan he had always wanted to be.

ᵒ❥ Your character and a friend reminisce about "the first time."

ᵒ❥ "Narcissism is the charge we make against people who aren't nearly so interested in us as we hoped they would be," your character says, or someone says to her.